To Jack Hardman ~

HURRY McMURRY

Enjoy!

Ann Chambers Noble

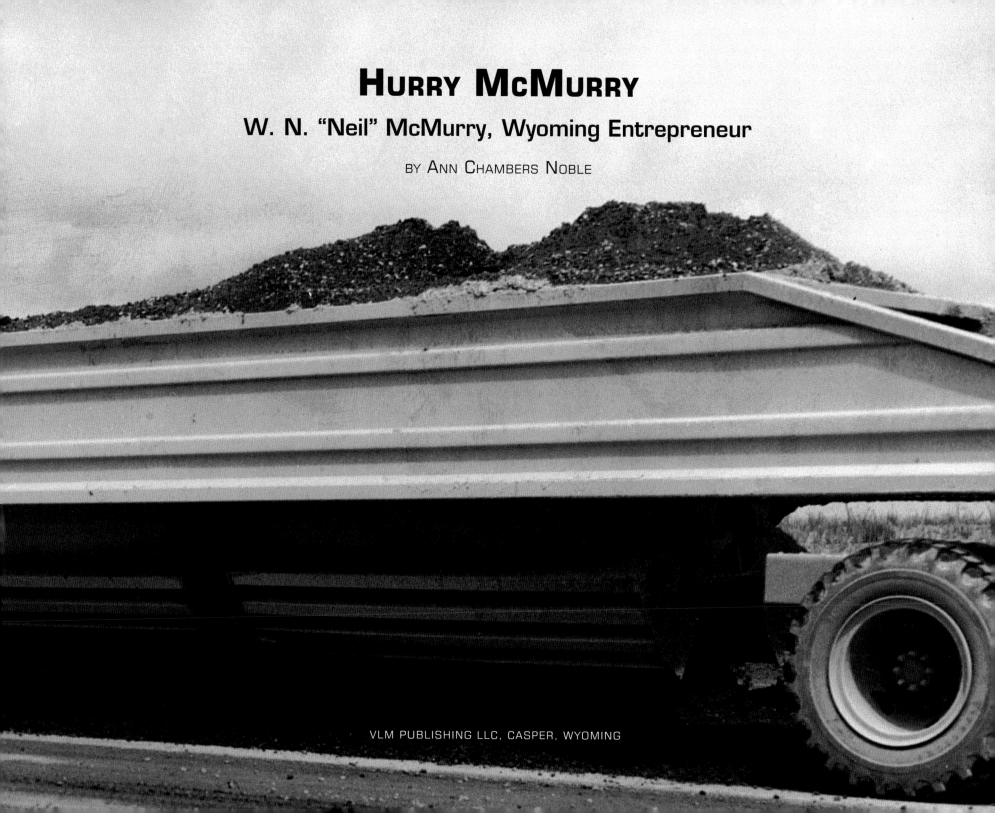

HURRY McMURRY

W. N. "Neil" McMurry, Wyoming Entrepreneur

BY ANN CHAMBERS NOBLE

VLM PUBLISHING LLC, CASPER, WYOMING

Hurry McMurry: W. N. "Neil" McMurry, Wyoming Entrepreneur
by Ann Chambers Noble

©2010 VLM Publishing LLC
5830 East Second Street
Casper, WY 82609
http://hurrymcmurry.com

ISBN-13: 978-0-615-37646-2
ISBN-10: 0615376460

Book and cover design by Sommers Studio, Pinedale, Wyoming
http://sommstudio.com

Frontispiece/title page photo: A Rissler and McMurry Company employee operates a Jersey spreader on the Interstate 80 job west of Cheyenne in 1962.

To our father, W. N. McMurry, a courageous man like all U.S. World War II veterans who did what they had to do to save the modern world, returned home and built a better America. To our mother, Ellie McMurry, who did what she had to do to protect, provide and love our growing family. To both of them who taught us lessons of working, giving and commitment.

— *Mick, Carol, Vic and Susan McMurry*

CONTENTS

Preface

"Some people dream of success ... While others wake up and work hard at it."
AUTHOR UNKNOWN

Entrepreneur: n. A person who organizes, operates and assumes the risk for business ventures.
AMERICAN HERITAGE DICTIONARY OF THE ENGLISH LANGUAGE

Several years ago, our brother, Victor, had the idea that we should write a book about the remarkable life of our father, William Neil McMurry. Of course, none of us knew anything about writing and publishing books, so after a couple of false starts, several years and lots of prodding and pushing by Victor, this book has finally become a reality.

To say that our father is an example of Tom Brokaw's "Greatest Generation" is an understatement. He was born in the 1920s, grew up in the Great Depression, and fought in World War II. The idea of the "Greatest Generation" may seem like a quaint idea to many of the younger generation. The reason that my siblings and I wanted to have this book written was so that the younger and future generations of our family will understand and have an appreciation of the hard work that was involved to provide the life we live today.

Neil McMurry provided us with a daily example of the value of hard work. He was up at 4 a.m., worked past sunset, and never stopped believing that you could do anything if you kept at it. At the age of eighty-seven he still believes in hard work and planning for the future. However, both our parents also taught us that it wasn't just about the money; it was also important to give back to the community you lived in. When you drive around Casper, Wyoming, you can see the impact he has had on that city. He is still making plans for his next improvements for Casper and the state.

All of us wish our sister Gayle had been here to participate in this book. We know she would have joined in with enthusiasm, and this makes us miss her all the more.

We would like to thank Ann Noble who helped us put this story on paper. Ann has graciously dealt with our individual personalities and schedules and has kept smiling throughout the entire process. She has also become a friend.

— *Carol McMurry*

INTRODUCTION

I was honored when Vic McMurry asked me, a historian, to assist him with compiling his father's life story. The project began as a biography intended for just family members, but as the research progressed, it became obvious that many people would be interested in Neil's life. Fortunately, Vic and the family are willing to share this book with the public.

There are many reasons to tell Neil McMurry's story. First, like other Wyomingites of his generation, Neil grew up during an extraordinary period in the history of the twentieth century. The story of his opportunities and challenges tells the story of Wyoming and the nation at this time.

Second, Neil is a true entrepreneur. He takes personal risks, assumes responsibility, and works incredibly hard. His business successes have positively impacted Wyoming and its citizens in many ways. Perhaps most important is how he succeeds: through honest business dealings. His handshake and his word are better than any written contract.

Given that we currently live in a post-recession era – arguably one of our nation's worst – which was brought on by unethical business practices, it is refreshing to read about a successful man with high moral standards for himself and those around him. We need to be reminded that there are those who have achieved their ambitions with their characters intact. Neil McMurry is proof that it can be done.

Neil also believes that with financial success, one has an obligation to give back. Neil's foresight, generosity, and philanthropy have directly benefited thousands of people, especially those whom he respects the most: the hard-working men and women of Wyoming. He is a role model for all.

— *Ann Chambers Noble*

Hurry McMurry

Center Street
Casper, Wyo.

Center Street in downtown Casper, Wyoming, in 1922, the year before Neil was born. The courthouse visible at the end of the street would later be moved to a different corner to allow Center Street to continue. Neil recalls that as a child he visited Santa Claus in the Iris building, seen at left. PHOTO BY BELL; MOKLER COLLECTION, CASPER COLLEGE WESTERN HISTORY CENTER

CHAPTER 1
YOUNG NEIL McMURRY

In early September 1923, Alma Doke McMurry went to visit her family's homestead twelve miles east of Greeley in the little town of Gill, Colorado. She went to see her father, who was ill. Although she was well along in her second pregnancy, by all accounts she did not return to Colorado intending to deliver her baby. But that is what happened, because the baby came early. William Neil McMurry was born September 12, 1923, at the Doke homestead attended by a doctor who arrived in a horse-drawn buggy.

Alma returned by train to her home in Casper, Wyoming, with her infant child, William Neil, six weeks old. Accompanying the child was something he would always regret – a Colorado birth certificate. For a man who would spend his life dedicated to Wyoming, the Colorado birth certificate seemed to ruin his otherwise perfect identity. Waiting in Casper for the mother and infant was the child's father, Otto Theodore McMurry, and the child's older brother Kenneth Doke McMurry, born in 1920.[1]

Casper in the 1920s was a bustling, industrialized cowtown, and Wyoming's second largest city. Incorporated in April 1889, Casper is the county seat for Natrona County. At 5,123 feet in altitude, it lies in the great bend on the south side of the North Platte River. South of the town the pine-covered slopes of Casper Mountain rise to an altitude of more than eight thousand feet. Casper developed into an industrial and commercial center for the state. Its basic industry was oil, but its geographic location at the juncture of four major highways and two mainline railroads would make it a key distribution point for a wide area. The town has always

Alma Doke McMurry, Neil's mother.

Neil's earliest photo.

With the First World War, the Salt Creek Oil Field spurred an oil boom in the Casper area. This is the view from 40 Mile Hill in 1923, when peak daily oil production reached 123,000 barrels a day. PHOTO BY BELL'S STUDIO; AMOCO REFINING CO. COLLECTION, CASPER COLLEGE WESTERN HISTORY CENTER

been surrounded by cattle ranching, with trails from the pastures of the CY Ranch becoming the streets of Casper. Cattle grazed practically in the shadows of oil refineries and storage tanks throughout the early twentieth century.

In 1890, the first oil well in the Casper area was drilled on the Salt Creek Field. And in 1895, the Pennsylvania Oil and Gas Company erected the first refinery in Wyoming near Casper. Demand for oil brought on by the First World War in 1916 precipitated the construction of two pipelines from Salt Creek to Casper, and set off a significant oil boom. A major player was the Midwest Oil Company, later swallowed up by the Standard Oil Company. The Casper Standard refinery, built in 1914, was one of the largest in the United States. The peak of the oil boom was reached late in 1917, though it continued throughout the 1920s. "Everyone was optimistic about the future of Wyoming's oil industry at the end of the First World War [1918]," wrote Wyoming historian T. A. Larson. "Everyone knew that the state had great oil reserves and that the multiplying automobiles would have to have gasoline."

"The boom pushed Casper into prominence," explained an author for the Federal Writer's Project in 1940. A local census in 1925 showed thirty thousand persons within the city limits and two thousand in the suburban refinery camps. "During the period of growth and free spending, the sky was the limit in Casper, and astounded residents of the former cow-town could see no limit to the rising value of waste lands and the free flow of capital. Hundreds of thousands of dollars were spent on luxurious hotels and office buildings. A million dollars was spent to build and equip a high school, and the municipal government launched a sweeping program of civic improvements. Residents saw Casper as the financial and industrial center of the Rocky Mountain region."[2]

Neil's father Otto and Uncle Vern McMurry hoped to take advantage of the oil boom in Casper when they left the family farm in Colorado in 1918 looking for work. Vern, the older brother, had served his country in uniform during World War I. Both brothers took employment with Standard Oil Company, though Vern soon quit and went to work at the Townsend Hotel, a luxury establishment. He subsequently left this job to work on the Cohn ranch in Leo, Wyoming, where he became foreman. Vern married the ranch owner's daughter and they had a baby girl. Unfortunately, the marriage ended; Vern then moved to Farson to start over in farming.

Otto McMurry remained at Standard Oil Company for his entire working career, making Casper his permanent home. Joining Kenneth and William Neil on July 7, 1927, was younger brother Donald Russell. A fourth son, Gary, died as an infant.

Otto performed shift work at Standard Oil Company. He made five dollars a day, which was an unusually high wage for the time nationally, but typical during the Wyoming oil boom of the 1920s. Otto wrote to his father telling him about his wage only to hear back from him that "no man in the world is worth five dollars a day!" Otto would retire in 1959, his last ten years at Standard Oil spent as a shift foreman.

Typical of quickly built boomtowns, Casper in the 1920s was a mixture of log cabins and derelict frame buildings shouldered next to newer brick structures. Its streets were wide and many were bordered with sentinel rows of cottonwoods and poplars, some of which still stand today.

Most middle- and upper-class people in the United States, particularly those in cities, enjoyed economic prosperity throughout the 1920s, as did the citizens of Casper due to the oil industry. Most of Wyoming, however, depended upon agriculture and coal mining and neither of these industries

This aerial view of the Standard Oil Refinery along the North Platte River in Casper was taken in 1920. Neil's father Otto spent his entire working life at this refinery, beginning in 1918.

BLACKMORE COLLECTION, CASPER COLLEGE WESTERN HISTORY CENTER

Otto and Alma McMurry's sons Donald, Kenneth, and Neil.

Neil attended McKinley School during his elementary school years, when he was called "Billy." Note the oil tanks in the distance at left.
CASPER COLLEGE WESTERN HISTORY CENTER

Jefferson School, first called East Casper School. Neil attended seventh grade here. WESTERN HISTORY COLLECTION, CASPER COLLEGE WESTERN HISTORY CENTER

fared well after World War I. While a severe drought throughout the West set agriculture back, coal prices sank and failed to come back up for nearly two decades. The final economic blow came with the stock market crash of 1929, sinking the state and Casper into further economic despair – this time with the rest of the nation.

William Neil McMurry spent his childhood and teen years in this uncertain economic climate. Neil's first home was a small tarpapered shack on Cherry Street on the west side of Casper, the only housing available in the 1920s boomtown. A few years later the family moved to a rented house at the end of Midwest Avenue, near where the road becomes Thirteenth Street. Then, in the early 1930s, Otto was able to move the family into a house at 424 South Melrose behind the hospital. Otto had purchased it for approximately thirteen hundred dollars after the previous owner's foreclosure. Neil recalls that the family who lost the home had children

Natrona County High School was constructed between 1924 and 1941 as a state-of-the-art school that Casper and Wyoming could be proud of. Neil attended from 1937 to 1941. STAFF COLLECTION, CASPER COLLEGE WESTERN HISTORY CENTER

in school with him, which was somewhat awkward.

Neil had started school at McKinley Elementary, but the family's mid-term move transferred him to Jefferson School. In the sixth grade William Neil, called "Billy," had his name changed to Neil by a teacher who had too many Billys in her class. By declaration, young McMurry was now to be called "Neil" for her convenience. Neil it would remain for the rest of his life.

Neil attended the seventh grade at Jefferson School, and the eighth grade in a separate building located next to the high school. In ninth grade, in 1937, he started at Natrona County High School (NCHS), the town's only high school. The cornerstone for the high school had been laid in 1924, and the school had opened in 1927, but the building was not completed until 1941. Construction began during the oil boom in Casper when money was plentiful and visions of grandeur were high. The school, costing one million dollars, has a dramatic entry tower with extensive terra cotta accents that highlight the Collegiate Gothic architectural style. It had numerous amenities unknown in Wyoming at that time, such as an indoor swimming pool. The physical appearance of NCHS, its conception, and its growth were closely intertwined with the economic growth of Casper and

Neil in high school.

the evolution of progressive ideas about education sweeping the country. When it was completed in 1941, it was one of the state's most distinctive high schools. Neil's graduating class in 1941 contained approximately three hundred students. Neil would be the first of three generations in his family to graduate from NCHS. His wife, Ellie, graduated a year after Neil in 1942. All five of their children – Carol, Mick, Vic, Gayle, and Susan – also graduated from this school, as did Vic's daughter Victoria.

Neil admits that even as a boy he did not like to be out of money. Given that it was the Great Depression, most people were out of money. Neil took his first job at age nine, delivering the *Denver Post* on Saturdays. A year later he was delivering the daily route for the same paper. In thirty days of delivering the *Denver Post* every morning, Neil could make three dollars – unless he got stiffed, which apparently was the case with at least one downtown business customer. Neil explains that he received twelve cents a month for every paper he delivered. If he collected from his subscribers, he would receive an additional five cents, but some people chose to pay the newspaper directly.

Neil kept his newspaper delivery jobs throughout high school, adding the *Casper Morning Star* route, too.

The Wyoming National Bank building in Casper, at the center of this view looking west on Durbin, was on Second Street at Durbin in the 1920s and 1930s. Neil opened a savings account at this bank so that he could save money to buy a car, which he did at age thirteen.

PHOTO BY TOM CARRIGEN; CHUCK MORRISON COLLECTION, CASPER COLLEGE WESTERN HISTORY CENTER, WYOMING STATE ARCHIVES, DEPARTMENT OF STATE PARKS AND CULTURAL RESOURCES.

Unfortunately, the different routes were not to the same houses. Neil never delivered the coveted evening paper, *The Casper Star-Tribune*, though. "You had to be a rich kid for that," he explains. Owner J. E. Hanway used to let the downtown businessmen's kids deliver his paper, because their fathers advertised with him.

An added bonus on the paper route came when Neil became the first guy in the morning to deliver newspapers to the Wigwam Bakery. The owner would reward the early bird with a sack of day-old rolls. Neil would get up at 4:30 a.m., build a fire in the wood stove and be the first one at the bakery to get the much-desired rolls "so when I came home the house was warm and everybody was glad to see me."

Neil also secured work at the Pop Service Station on the corner of Ash and Midwest. Neil would fill customer vehicles with gasoline and wash their windshields. He would also sell motor oil for ten cents a quart. This motor oil was likely crude oil from the Fall Creek Oil Field and was a beautiful green color. Neil occasionally helped the owner "Pop" add lead and color to his gasoline, though Pop did not have a set formula, resulting in great variations in the product. "Sometimes it was bright red and other times it was pink," says Neil. The customers did not seem to mind, probably because Pop had cheap gas.

One of Neil's least favorite childhood jobs was working at a grocery store in North Casper on Saturdays for ten cents an hour. The work usually involved cleaning out the cases: unpleasant for a restless young man.

It was while Neil was delivering newspapers, around age ten or eleven, that he realized he wanted a car to be able to deliver yet more newspapers. Drivers' licenses were not yet required, and there was no minimum age for driving. Neil opened a savings account at Wyoming National Bank in downtown Casper and added a dollar or two whenever he

Neil at center, with neighbor Thayne Middaugh at left and Pete Anderson at right. The three young men are standing outside of the Middaugh home in Casper, admiring Neil's 1928 Model A Roadster, prior to its new paint job.

Neil sitting on his 1928 Model A Roadster in the driveway of 424 South Melrose, after painting it Hong Kong yellow with black fenders. Neil says he "sweated bullets getting the old paint off." This car was equipped with exhaust pipe whistles until the police made him take them off.

made a racket!" recalls Neil. "When I'd leave school I'd open them up and everybody knew I was going!" One day Neil came home to find a policeman waiting with his father. The officer asked Neil, "Are you the kid with the exhaust whistles?" Neil admitted he was. "Take them off," ordered the law officer. And that was the end of Neil's exhaust whistles.

Regarding school Neil confesses, "I had no desire to learn, and I regret that. I didn't pay any attention in class. They tried to teach me and I refused to learn and I won, unfortunately. And I had so many jobs, sometimes late at night, that I'd sleep in school." One teacher told him, "Neil, you have the highest I.Q. of anybody in this class and you have the poorest grades." Neil admits he lacked academic moti-

could. By the time he was thirteen years old, in 1937, Neil had saved seventy-five dollars. With the money, Neil purchased a used 1928 Model A Roadster for fifty-five dollars; another twenty went for trinkets and paint. "It wasn't in very good shape," Neil admits. He overhauled the engine. "I figured it out. It was so simple anyone could do it." He also took a putty knife and a blowtorch and scraped off all the paint, sanded it down, and painted it Hong Kong yellow with black fenders. "It was the sportiest thing in town," says Neil. "I put a set of exhaust whistles on it." These objects made a loud whistle when they were put on the exhaust pipes. "Holy bucket, they

vation. "I said 'I'm going to be a working guy, what the hell do I need U.S. History or English Lit for?'" Neil recalls being sent to the school counselor, Mr. Scott. He asked Neil what he wanted to do. Looking out the window at the Northwest Railyard where workers were switching an engine, Neil told the counselor he wanted to do that, having no intention of doing so. Mr. Scott said he would get Neil an apprentice job at the railyard, but Neil never followed through with it. He just wanted out of school to have time to get a real job and start making more money. "They gave me a high school diploma anyway," says Neil.

"It was a good childhood, even if it was a little bit barren," Neil recalls years later, referring to the lack of material goods. "You didn't notice, because everyone was broke." The McMurrys may have been better off than some because Otto was able to maintain employment throughout the Great Depression, although with a cut in hours and wages. To feed the family on a tight budget, Otto visited his cousin in Basin, Wyoming, where he was able to secure hundred-pound sacks of potatoes and beans. Neil claims his father also brought home horse bran one year, and vows to never eat that again. "We ate good enough," says Neil. "We had a house. In those days, everyone was in about the same shape, or worse. You didn't really feel sorry for yourself."

Reflecting back, Neil appreciates that his parents enabled him to have a good childhood during hard economic times. His father was a kind, hard-working gentleman, always available to his family. His mother, too, was kind and family-oriented. Alma had a great love for books. "She would take us to the library and come home with a bunch of books," recalls Neil. "A week later she would take them back and get a new batch." Neil also remembers his mother as "pretty laid-back." He illustrates the point by describing how she would let the boys work on their bikes in the front room of the house where there was linoleum on the floor. She also permitted her dining room table and a blanket to double as a fort in their cowboys and Indians games. At day's end, though, all was cleaned up and their house returned to order.

Neil's childhood in Casper during the Great Depression clearly influenced the man he became. He enjoyed love and support from smart, hard-working parents. He was an ambitious child willing to work for what he wanted. While jobs were scarce and paid little, Neil still found employment, opened a banking account, and owned a car – all by age thirteen. By his own admission he would be given a high school diploma which he had not necessarily earned, yet his education in the business world had already begun.

Neil, at right, rabbit hunting with his younger brother Donald. All three of the McMurry boys were short, but Neil was always the shortest. "The other two grew up, but not me," Neil likes to say.

Chapter 2
The World at War: Neil's Generation

The radio in the McMurry house was not working on September 1, 1939, but the world news was critical enough for Otto to sit in his 1934 Ford, parked in the driveway, to listen on the car radio. "This can't be good," he would later tell his sons. "This means you're going to war." Otto was right.

Adolph Hitler released his "blitzkrieg," or lightning war, on Poland that day, a swift and massive invasion of that country. Poland was first attacked by the German Luftwaffe, or air force, followed quickly with ground forces. Within days, Poland surrendered to Germany and World War II was underway. Within months, Germany had invaded and conquered Denmark, Norway, and France. Italy joined forces with Germany, forming the Axis Powers, which moved south into Africa. Within three months, the only remaining European country not under Axis control was Great Britain.

The Luftwaffe began its bombardment of the British Isles in July 1940, with Germany expecting to control London within two months. Dubbed the Battle of Britain, the intense airborne engagement instead continued until October 1940, and is considered one of the turning points of the war. German planes outnumbered those of the Royal Air Force, but the British had better planes and pilots. They shot down so many aircraft that the Germans were forced to give

Facing page: Leaving gray contrails in their wake, B-17 Flying Fortresses persevere through a dense curtain of anti-aircraft fire, or "flak", on their way to bomb oil targets in Germany in December, 1944. The white cloud at top is all that remains of a B-17 that was hit. ©BETTMANN/CORBIS

Neil in uniform, late 1944.

Clockwise from top left: Elnora "Ellie" Mc Gregor in high school; Ellie with her mother Stella at center and younger sister Mary Lou; Ellie with brother Dick.

up daylight attacks. The British used a new invention, and a carefully guarded secret – radar – to track the attacking planes.

While war raged, Neil McMurry was finishing his high school years in Casper. The United States was not yet formally participating in the war, but American industries were actively building military armaments. Neil had a friend who had secured a war job in San Diego, but who had left his Ford Model A in Casper. He asked Neil to bring the car down to him and then stay to work. Anxious to leave Casper for the first time, Neil agreed to leave as soon as he graduated in the Spring of 1941. "My dad cried when I left," recalls Neil. "But I was bound and determined to see what was out there since I had never been out of Casper."

The Allies concentrated on developing bombers that could fly long distances. By 1942, the Allied air forces were making as many as one thousand bomber raids per day on mainland Europe against German targets. This critical air war would play a major role in the Allied victory. It would also be an important event in Neil's life.

American volunteer pilots had flown with the Royal Air Force from the beginning of hostilities in 1939. They began participating as full allies when the United States joined the war on December 8, 1941. The United States Eighth Air Force would be stationed in England and fly B-17 Flying Fortress and B-24 Liberator heavy bombers, as well as Thunderbolt, Lightning, and Mustang fighters. The Allied strategic air forces would attack Axis military and industrial targets.

Meanwhile, in San Diego during the summer of 1941, Neil tried unsuccessfully to get hired at an airplane factory. He was turned away because he was only seventeen years old, and had to take any odd job he could find. Finally, upon turning eighteen in September, Neil was hired by Consolidated Aircraft, which later merged with Douglas Aircraft Company. The company was building U.S. Navy PBY flying boats, an amphibious aircraft. "PB" stood for "Patrol Bomber," and "Y" was the code letter designated for Consolidated Aircraft. Neil took the only job available, which was working as a clerk. This was not satisfactory for the high-energy young man. "I'm not really an office guy," explains Neil. He never would be.

Then came the bombing of Pearl Harbor on December 7, 1941. Like so many young men at that time, Neil immediately tried to sign up with the U.S. Army. He had seen a squadron of P-38s, flying over California to quell concerns that the Japanese were going to bomb North Island. "I've got to fly one of them," thought Neil. With a lot of men ahead of him in the line at San Diego, he was initially turned away. Five months would pass before Neil would be inducted into the United States Army on April 30, 1942.

Neil returned to Wyoming waiting to report for military service. "I came home and the army didn't call me and they didn't call me," explains Neil. It gave him a chance to spend more time with his high school sweetheart, Elnora Jean McGregor. Affectionately called "Ellie," Elnora was born on August 20, 1924, in Sargent, Nebraska, to Hugh and Stella McGregor.[1] Ellie's family moved to Casper when she was two years old. Her father was an auto mechanic for a Ford garage, then later worked for Ringsby Trucking Company. Ellie was the third child of six, with three brothers and two sisters. The oldest was Victor followed by another brother, Dean, then Elnora and her younger

Clockwise from top left: Ellie on high school graduation day; wedding photo of Ellie's parents, Hugh and Stella McGregor; Neil and Ellie; Ellie as a young woman. Of this photo, Neil says, "She was a good gal. She is responsible for the success of my children. She raised them."

Neil and Ellie's wedding day.

Ellie and Neil near her aunt and uncle's bar in Evansville, where they went to celebrate the night they were married.

Ellie and Neil were married July 11, 1942, in the minister's chambers at the First Presbyterian Church in Casper (built in 1925).

WESTERN HISTORY COLLECTION, CASPER COLLEGE WESTERN HISTORY CENTER

siblings Mary Lou, Francis, and Richard. Although her father worked, the McGregor family was not able to afford indoor plumbing until she was in high school. This was typical of the times in her neighborhood, known as "North Casper," where the Great Depression wages were very low and most of the houses lacked indoor water or plumbing.

Neil and Ellie had started spending time together when she was a freshman at Natrona County High School and he was a sophomore. Ellie later told of a time when Neil was leaning back in his chair at school in an attempt to get her attention, and he succeeded when he fell backwards, hitting his head. "She was nice," recalls Neil, "real nice." Throughout the years, many others would describe Ellie the same way.

Ellie was not particularly studious in school, preferring to spend time with her girlfriends or with Neil. She later admitted to her children that sometimes a date with Neil included buying quarts of beer and drinking them in his car. In these years of school uniforms and strict rules, Ellie and her friends used to try to show their independence by rolling their stockings down during their long cold walk to school, stopping at the Burlington Train Station to get warm.

Typical of her time, Ellie wanted to be married and have children. The uncertainty of the war years charged these feelings with a sense of urgency. Men and women recognized the unfortunate reality that many young soldiers would never return. On July 11, 1942, Ellie and Neil were married. Ellie was one month shy of her eighteenth birthday and had just graduated from high school. Neil was only a year older. Their wedding was a private, quiet affair, common for the war years and the economic conditions. They were married in the Presbyterian Church on Eighth South and Wolcott Street in the minister's chambers with both sets of parents in attendance. It was an evening ceremony, after Neil had worked all day. While on the job, a pneumatic tamper

Ellie and Neil as newlyweds in Whittier, California.

Neil and Ellie lived in Santa Ana, California, while Neil was a cadet.

In California, Ellie took a riveting job in an airplane factory while Neil was training as a cadet. Here, Ellie (at left) and her friend Jackie are ready to go to work for the war effort.

machine had run over Neil's big toe, causing him great pain and making him limp at his wedding. Following the simple service, the parents and newlyweds celebrated at the Road Side Inn, an establishment owned by Ellie's aunt and uncle. Years later Neil recalls the post-wedding party when they got "drunker than hell!"

Still not called up by the armed forces, Neil quickly found work in Casper. The U.S. Army was building an air base on the outskirts of town, and he hired on with the contractor paving the runways. When the job was completed in the fall, Neil was laid off.

Neil went to the Casper unemployment office, where he was told that work was available with Western Geophysical on a seismograph crew. "I showed up to work wearing heavy clothes, gloves, and boots," recalls Neil. The other fellows

These two photos of Neil were taken at Avon Park Army Air Field in Florida, where he received phase and gunner training for B-17 Flying Fortress aircraft in 1943.

seeking the same job were not wearing outdoor gear. Neil was hired. The company needed to move to Whittier, California, in the winter of 1942, so Neil drove a company truck to make the trip. Not unusual for Wyoming, it was a bitterly cold winter. The truck Neil was driving had come from Texas and had no heater. He used a scraper and a blowtorch to keep the windshield clear. At one point, he set the blowtorch down on the floor, and burned a hole in his Levi's! When Neil got to Lyman, Wyoming, it was 40 degrees below zero. The next morning, the truck would not start – nor would any other vehicle.

While Neil was in California working on the seismograph crew, Ellie decided to come out to live with her new husband. Ellie's first trip out of Casper was riding a bus by herself to California. She arrived just before Christmas, only to immediately return home to attend her eldest brother's funeral. Victor McGregor had been killed in Pueblo, Colorado, while training with the army in a B-24 bomber.

After the funeral, Ellie returned to California "about the time they called me into the cadet [training] program," Neil recalls. He reported for duty in Santa Ana. In nearby Long Beach, the Douglas Aircraft Company had an airplane factory where Ellie secured a job operating a rivet gun in the tail section of bombers – a real "Rosie the Riveter."[2] As a small woman, she fit into the tight work space. For these few months the young newlyweds lived in Whittier.

Unfortunately for Neil, his desire to become a pilot was soon dashed. The army was experiencing a surplus of pilot school applicants at this time, so he was sent instead to gunnery school, where there was a shortage of applicants. In early 1943, he went for training in Denver, Colorado. Ellie returned to Casper, where she lived part-time with her folks and part-time with Neil's family.

Neil went to Buckley and Lowry Fields near Denver for Army Air Corps Technical Training School, a program that prepared air crews for the B-17 Flying Fortress. It was here he met Ray McMillan and Jim McNeil, friends he would keep for life. The army organized everyone in alphabetical order, so these men were always next to McMurry in identification line up, mail call, and eventually, in the formation of bomber crews. When Neil was given a pass to get off base, he would visit an aunt and uncle in Denver. Jim McNeil recalls years later that Neil included him on these visits.

In the fall of 1943, after completing his initial training in Colorado, Neil made a quick trip home to Casper to see Ellie and his family. He was then sent to Florida for additional instruction at Fort Myers Army Air Base and Avon Park Army Air Field, the training grounds for B-17 aircraft crews. The soldiers were put through phase training, in which each serviceman was instructed in various phases, or areas, including mechanics, armaments, and gunnery. Everyone was taught to operate a machine gun. Neil was trained as an armament gunner, putting the bombs on the planes and arming them. This was the final training prior to combat.

After Avon Park, Neil and his fellow soldiers took a train to New York, boarded the Queen Elizabeth, and headed to

Laundry day at Avon Park, Florida. Ellie joined Neil there while he was training in the fall of 1943.

war. The ship traveled unescorted, which was frightening for the servicemen, even though the ship was faster than the enemy submarines. There was always the chance the giant ship would show up on an enemy's periscope. For six days Neil and the other soldiers stayed in the hold of the ship. They were allowed above waterline and in the fresh air to eat meals and to exercise once a day. Neil recalls only the cold boiled potatoes the British crew fed them. He also remembers having to shave with cold saltwater. "Thank God I didn't have much of a beard," remarks Neil. A large Englishman stood by the hatch to the bottom hold. Neil asked him once, "Just what is your job, fella?" The man explained that if the ship took a torpedo, it was his responsibility to close the hatch. "What about us?" inquired Neil. "Gotta save the ship," the man replied.

Six days after leaving the United States, the ship landed safely in Ireland. The crews were then taken to England, the staging ground for the European air assault. Air battles were still critical to the war, though by now the Allies were on the offensive.

Neil and his fellow recruits would become part of a massive coordinated military effort between the British and Americans against the Germans. At this point in the war, the fall of 1943, the British Royal Air Force Bomber Command favored saturation bombing at night. This technique meant dropping a large load of bombs in the general area of a target, gambling that enough bombs would hit the location and

Top left: Neil's B-17 crew in England waits to take off on a mission. Note airplane in the background. Left to right: unnamed pilot, Rios, Wimset, co-pilot Grimkowski, Raymond McMillan, unknown, Simonton, and Neil at far right.

Bottom left: Back row – Berry, Simonton, and Neil. Front row – Rios, McMillan, and Wimset.

A group of B-17 Flying Fortresses flies over Germany on its way to bomb Stuttgart, September 6, 1943.
©CORBIS

any one time, two thousand aircraft were in the air.

When Neil and his group of fresh soldiers arrived, they were placed with experienced squadrons, filling positions of soldiers injured or killed during previous missions.

The B-17 was a heavy bomber that was not pressurized, making it necessary for all the crew members to wear oxygen masks during all their flights above ten thousand feet. It was not heated, requiring the crew to wear heavy insulated outer clothing to protect them from temperatures reaching sixty-five degrees below zero. The plane carried little armor but was mounted with eleven 50-caliber machine guns. The normal bomb load on the B-17 was five to eight thousand pounds, dropped while the plane traveled at 170 miles per hour. During the course of the war, these bombers flew over 290,000 sorties and delivered over 640,000 tons of bombs.

destroy it. The U.S. Eighth Air Force favored pinpoint bombing. This strategy involved dropping bombs on important targets from high altitudes by daylight. Instead of attempting to destroy entire industries, the Allies tried to knock out key targets. For example, bombers destroyed dams in the Ruhr Valley, depriving many German industries of their power sources. They also hit ball-bearing plants, slowing down the production of machinery, aircraft, and tanks. At

The B-17 bomber was cramped, gusty, noisy, cold, and like all military weapon systems, a dangerous place to be. Missions were long and uncomfortable. The B-17 crew numbered ten: pilot, co-pilot, navigator, bombardier/nose gunner, flight engineer/top turret gunner, radio operator, two waist gunners, ball turret gunner, and tail gunner. Neil would work various gunner positions.

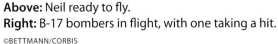

Above: Neil ready to fly.
Right: B-17 bombers in flight, with one taking a hit.

©BETTMANN/CORBIS

All the gunners were responsible for defending the aircraft. The waist gunners stood at the sides of the plane. The tail gunner was likely in the most strategic location to deter enemy aircraft, because enemy pilots tended to attack the rear of B-17 formations, starting with the last plane, and working their way forward. The tail gunner would make his way to his position by crawling through a long, narrow passageway to the very rear of the aircraft after the plane had taken off. He held a kneeling position and manned a twin machine gun system.

The "belly" or ball turret gunner was always the smallest man, because this firing position had the smallest space. Located midway back from the nose of the aircraft, it was a glass dome or turret projecting from the belly of the plane, with a diameter of about three feet. Inside the plane, above the dome, was a hatch that a very small man could just barely get through. Crawling in, the gunner had to latch the hatch, which would then allow the turret to rotate 360 degrees. His job was to protect the plane from attacks below. If the plane were hit, his chances of getting out of the turret were

A Flying Fortress takes off from an air force base in England in September 1942. The ball turret beneath the plane is visible just behind the wings.
©BETTMANN/CORBIS

While stationed in England in 1944, Neil received this photo from Ellie, pregnant with their first child, Carol.

not very good. Not surprisingly, the highest casualty rates on the B-17s were the ball turret gunners. All eleven guns on the plane fired at a rate of thirteen rounds per second and had a total supply of ammunition lasting one minute. The gunners needed to be good shots.

On Neil's early missions he served as a waist gunner, but soon he moved to other positions. As Neil explains it, "I was in the waist and then we lost the tail gunner so I went to the tail. Then we lost the ball turret gunner – I'm not sure that he wasn't just put into jail, he was kind of a renegade – so I went to the ball. I spent over half of my missions in the ball, which wasn't a very nice place to be. You have to turn the guns down, crawl up in the waist, find your chest pack [parachute], and try to get it hooked on. If the airplane was hit, you didn't have a chance." Neil's small size kept him in the ball for most of his missions.

All the crew members experienced extreme stress when flying bombing missions. The gunners, as defenders of the plane and crew, were always anticipating the next attack by enemy aircraft. The suspense was almost harder to endure than the heat of battle.

Neil flew with the 385th Bomb Group stationed at Great Ashfield, England. This group would ultimately fly 296 missions and sustain 129 losses. The American crews were accustomed to 3 a.m. briefings about their bomber missions, including routes and targets. The crews were then prepared to take off at daylight. Neil's group, assigned to Ipswitch, bombed points in Germany and France. They also bombed a heavy water installation in Norway to disrupt German work on the nuclear bomb.

Neil's first mission was to Hahn, Germany. "I decided right then I was not going to enjoy this." From the air, Neil witnessed horrible casualties. One time he saw an airman jumping from a burning plane. Tragically, the flames engulfed his parachute. Another time Neil watched as an airman from another plane pulled his chute release too quickly, and his parachute caught on the tail of the plane. Nearby bombers, as well as his own, were constantly under fire. Other planes took hits, sometimes crashing to the ground. Neil was also painfully aware of civilian casualties. Although the bomber missions were to strike military targets only, their early form of radar, known as the pathfinder, did not necessarily pinpoint exact military sites. Neil sometimes wondered if women and children were hit on the Allied bombing missions, which "always bothered me."

"One time the front of the plane was on fire," recalls Neil. "We were standing at the door with our chutes, ready to jump – we were over Stuttgart. I thought I better check before I jumped. The people down there weren't happy with us – we had bombed the hell out of them. When our guys bailed in Germany, big crowds gathered on them and treated them bad. I didn't think I wanted to be down there, but it looked better than being in a burning airplane with five thousand pounds of bombs. I fought back in and checked with the pilots, who were screaming, 'Don't jump! Don't jump!' They got the fire out."

On one mission in which Neil served as the tail gunner, bullets pierced the back of the airplane. Wind blew through the sizable bullet holes at temperatures of 55 to 60 degrees below zero, right onto Neil. By the time the plane landed, both of Neil's ears were seriously frostbitten. His injuries resulted in Neil being grounded – and being awarded a Purple Heart!

In August 1944, while Neil was on the ground recovering from frostbite, his group of Allied bombers hammered at the rich oil fields of Ploesti, Romania, in the attack that finally stopped production there. Black smoke billowed for miles as the Allied bombs ignited the oil. Although he missed this spectacular event, Neil remembers seeing many other black-smoke fires from bombed oil refineries.

This family portrait with daughter Carol was taken in Casper while Neil was on furlough.

A few days prior to the June 6, 1944, Allied invasion of the European mainland, known to history by its military name of D-Day, Neil's group was sent to France loaded with arms. Its mission was to fly down the Rouen Valley to drop guns and ammunition in metal cylinders with parachutes to the free French to assist them as a fifth column, or internal army, against the Germans. Flying only a few hundred feet above the ground, the crew could easily see the civilians waving at them. Neil had a box of francs, the French currency, that he sent down to the partisans. "I really liked that mission," recalls Neil.

On this particular mission, half of the group, including Neil, returned to England for refueling and rearmament. The other half bombed Poland and went on to Russia to refuel and rearm, with plans to bomb again coming back. After landing in Russia, the American planes were destroyed by German fighters that had followed them there. Russian women tried to put out the fires on the burning planes using their straw brooms. The stranded crews eventually returned to England, but without much support from the Russians and their government.

On D-Day itself, Neil flew two missions. Neil's group bombed the beaches just ahead of the initial Allied landing at Normandy. That afternoon, when the Americans had gained a small beachhead, Neil's group bombed behind the enemy line. The missions continued for days. On July 25, 1944, Neil's group was ordered to bomb in front of the yellow smoke that marked the location of Allied troops. Tragically, by the time the bombers arrived, wind had caused the smoke to drift back, and there was no communication to the airplanes explaining the shift. As a result, bombs hit American targets, including General Lesley J. McNair, the highest-ranking American to be killed in action in World War II.

Neil's crew members remember having a drink or two (at least) after their stressful missions. Neil would join them. But when the guys later went to town to find entertainment with women, they remember Neil returning to the barracks alone. He was always faithful to Ellie.

By September 1944, bomber crews for B-17s were being reorganized due to numerous plane and crew casualties. Gunners were given the option to stay for additional missions, or return to the United States and wait to be sent to the Pacific War. By now Neil had flown twenty-nine missions, only one short of getting a DFC, or Distinguished Flying Cross. The company clerk came to Neil and offered him the opportunity to get in one more mission to earn the award. Neil would have nothing of it. He was taking any opportunity to get back to the United States.

This time aboard the Queen Elizabeth II, Neil returned to America, arriving in early September 1944 at Camp Myles Standish in Taunton, outside of Boston, Massachusetts. The U.S. Army Red Cross had notified Neil just before leaving England that Ellie had had their first child, a baby girl named Carol Jean. Actually, Neil was the second McMurry to be informed of Carol's arrival. Neil's brother Kenneth was in the armed services in the northern countries of Newfoundland, Greenland, and Iceland. His Captain had called him and said, "Congratulations! You have a seven-pound baby daughter!" He said, "Great! But I'm not married and haven't been to the States in two years!" He knew it was Neil's baby. Neil was allowed to immediately leave the camp on furlough, but did not tell Ellie he was coming. He wanted to surprise her. He was so anxious to get home he even took a cab from the Casper bus stop, a big expense during tight economic times. It was a highly emotional reunion for both of them.

Neil's parents kept the baby for a couple of weeks, enabling Neil and Ellie to go to Santa Ana, California for some rest and time together. Ellie returned to Casper when Neil

Top left: The family at home in November 1944, at 424 South Melrose in Casper. Left to right: Neil's mother Alma, Neil holding Carol, Ellie, and Neil's father Otto. **Top right:** Ellie stands in front of Otto's 1937 Ford in Casper.

was called back to duty in Texas. "There really wasn't a lot of use for old gunners. You know, they didn't have many skills," claims Neil. "We were just killing time waiting to go to the Japanese theater." At one point, Neil was sent to Arlington, Texas, and Ellie visited him there.

While in Texas, Neil reunited with Jim McNeil, who had trained with him in Colorado and also had flown in B-17 missions from England. In Texas they waited to be shipped out to serve in the Pacific War. Like Neil, Jim was married while in the service.

"We were just getting ready to ship to Japan when they dropped the bomb that saved us," says Neil. He is referring to the atomic bombs dropped on Hiroshima and Nagasaki,

which quickly resulted in Japan's unconditional surrender. This action canceled the long-anticipated and dreaded invasion of the Japanese mainland. "There's a lot of controversy about that, but if you had been in my position sitting there to go back to combat, you'd be glad, too. The invasion would have been a bloody mess."

Equally anxious for Neil to be home were his young wife, Ellie, and their baby girl. As with any veteran, the trauma of the war experience would remain with Neil, but he was able to keep it from being apparent. To assist the transition to civilian life, Neil quickly immersed himself in his work. He would keep up his hard working, long days on the job his entire life.

CHAPTER 3
RESERVOIRS, HIGHWAYS, BRIDGES, AND INTERSTATES: THE RISSLER AND MCMURRY COMPANY

Neil McMurry was honorably discharged from the U.S. Army and returned permanently to Casper, Wyoming, in September 1945. He had just turned twenty-two years old. Waiting for him was his wife, pregnant again, and their one-year-old daughter. "We didn't have a car, a house, or clothes," remembers Neil. Securing employment to support his young family was his immediate concern. "There were fifteen million guys just like me bucking for a place to get a foot in the door," recalls Neil, referring to the other returning war veterans. "I didn't have any education. I didn't have any skills. All I had was my time. So that's what I gave them."

Vern E. Rissler had grown up on a ranch west of Casper. Vern's father had purchased a D4 Caterpillar bulldozer for ranch use, but during the lean financial years of the 1930s and World War II, the Risslers supplemented the ranch income with earth moving work using the bulldozer. "By 1946, Vern had pushed enough dirt and saved enough money to buy his father out," reported the *Casper Star-Tribune* fifty years later.[1]

Neil's uncle, Horace McMurry, was working for Vern Rissler when Neil returned to Casper. Another man had recently quit, so Horace, nicknamed "Punk,"

Facing Page: Rissler and McMurry Company equipment moves rock in a quarry near Vedauwoo between Laramie and Cheyenne in 1962.

Caterpillar Tractor Company photographed Neil on a job stripping overburden at a uranium mining operation east of Riverton in November 1957. Rissler and McMurry Company was using Caterpillar equipment on the site. TEEN BECKSTED PHOTO

Vern Rissler. CASPER STAR-TRIBUNE COLLECTION, CASPER COLLEGE WESTERN HISTORY CENTER

introduced Neil to Vern as a possible replacement. Vern hired Neil to keep the bulldozer running longer hours. Neil recalls that Rissler "didn't show a lot of signs of prosperity, and I remember Ellie asking me, 'Are you sure he can pay you?' I said, 'I don't know, but I hope so!'" In the immediate post-war years, the United States was transitioning from a war-time to a peacetime economy. New jobs were being created,

but not at a pace to keep up with the high number of return-ing veterans flooding the job market. Neil has always deeply appreciated Vern for giving him a job during this period.

Throughout the war the military had priority on all equip-ment built in the country. With the war over in 1945, the U.S. Army released equipment for civilian use. This enabled Vern to purchase a new D6 Caterpillar bulldozer. Rissler also had an old 1935 DS35 International truck "that wasn't much of a horse," remembers Neil. It was used to pull a tank of fuel.

For jobs away from home, which was most of the time, Rissler provided living quarters in an old trailer, a sheep wagon, and a worn-out White truck with a "house" over the steering wheel. Neil stayed alone in the sheep wagon. Neil's shift started at midnight, so he slept during the day. He stayed alone to avoid noise from fellow workers coming into the trailer. "We provided the meat ourselves. We ate a lot of deer and a lot of antelope." Neil also remembers the time when he shot an elk, but sheep dogs, protecting a nearby flock, ate most of it.

Neil was not the only one on the lonely Wyoming prai-rie recently home from World War II. Neil recalled one time shortly after the war when they were working in the Big Horn Basin. Neil had shot a dry elk cow about dusk. One of the crew members had a French nephew with him who had recently arrived from France, where he had been a German prisoner of war. Having been nearly starved in captivity, he was somewhat obsessed with food, so Neil shared with him a hindquarter of the elk. Headlights appeared on the horizon, alarming the nephew, who did not speak English. Neil remembers the young man yelling, "Gestapo! Gestapo!" almost out of his mind with fear.

Neil's living accommodations "upgraded" in late 1947 when Vern bought an old city bus, covered up the win-dows, and built bunk beds and cabinets. It may have been

Wyoming's first "recreational vehicle," though it was used only for work. "It was all very crude," explains Neil, "but enough for construction guys. We 'poor-boyed' everything cause that's the way you had to do it when you didn't have any money."

Rissler took any earth-moving work he could get anywhere around the state. Neil remembers a summer in the Big Horn Basin early in his career when he would knock on doors, offering dirt-moving services. Soon he was cleaning out corrals, leveling land, and digging ditches. This work helped supplement their jobs building reservoir dams.

In the 1940s, the federal government sponsored a program to build or subsidize the construction of reservoir dams for ranchers in the interest of soil conservation and providing livestock water. The Bureau of Land Management funded reservoirs on land it managed, and on private land the federal government paid half the cost if the rancher

Neil's then-brother-in-law John Fogle holding the rifle, Neil, and Hugh McGregor at right. This was about 1947 at a job near Lost Cabin, while Neil was working for Vern and before he became a partner. Neil says, "I was working up there for a rancher, and Ellie came up on Sundays with the kids and a case of beer."

paid the balance. The program was ultimately turned over to the Soil Conservation Service in the Department of Agriculture. Wyoming ranchers were taking advantage of this program, providing a lot of work for Vern and Neil.

Rissler and McMurry guaranteed their reservoirs, unless the water overflowed it. If the water went out underneath, they would always fix it. Neil avoided reservoir problems by getting rid of all the vegetation, digging down to good, solid dirt, then putting good, solid dirt back in. Neil estimates

that at least 90 percent of these reservoirs are still in use on ranches today, having seen several of them from an airplane years later. "It was a great government program," says Neil. "It stopped erosion, utilized the range, and cows didn't have to walk as far to water. It was a boon to the country."

In order to pay for the new equipment, Vern, Neil, and Neil's Uncle Punk ran the bulldozer around the clock. Punk did not work fast, especially compared to Neil, and did not appreciate Neil pushing him to work harder. Trying to save

Ellie visits a job site with young Mick, and Neil at center. Note most of the men are wearing some form of cowboy hat. "Our hard hats in those days," explains Neil.

time, Neil would even fix dinner for Punk, then service the bulldozer while Punk ate. Eventually Punk quit, telling Rissler, "I can't take that kid [Neil] anymore." Punk went on to work for Continental Oil in Glenrock, retiring at age sixty-two.

Vern paid three cents to move a yard of dirt, with the income split between Neil and Punk, a penny and a half each. When Punk quit, Neil suggested to Vern that the two of them continue to work around the clock, which they did.

Neil recalls the company grossed $45,000 to $48,000 a year by the late 1940s. This was good income for the day, but it required very long days. "I would run from 4 a.m. until 8 or 9 p.m.," remembers Neil. "I would go look for work, survey a dam, or get some diesel and supplies and haul them with my pickup. Sometimes I would keep the dozer going while the other guys ate. I kept the equipment going twenty-four hours a day. I got in plenty of hours." Neil obviously did not need a lot of sleep. The hard work was paying off. "I made some pretty fair money."

While Neil was putting in his atrociously long hours working, Ellie was home alone taking care of the children. Fortunately, she had her parents and Neil's folks to assist with the childcare and household responsibilities. When Neil

Vern Rissler's trailer was used for housing on jobs away from home. Neil usually stayed in a sheep wagon pulled behind.

did come home, it never was for long. He seemed to always find work to do.

Neil and Vern were never formally trained in heavy equipment operation or business. "Most of their education came from hard knocks, just from getting in there and trying it," comments Jim Rissler, Vern's son. "There was no limit on their desire to grow."

At the end of 1947, Vern and Neil bought a tractor together. They operated the new tractor along with Vern's older one, enabling them to take on more work. On January 2, 1949, they entered into a formal partnership and the Rissler and McMurry Company was born. "I've always appreciated Vern giving me the opportunity for the partnership," says Neil. "I'm forever grateful for that." The Rissler and McMurry Company would become one of the largest Wyoming-owned highway construction companies in the state.

By the early 1950s, funds supporting reservoir work ceased, motivating Neil and Vern to look elsewhere for jobs.

Vern and Neil worked with the Rissler family's D4 Caterpillar bulldozer in the early years of their association. This bulldozer had helped supplement the family's ranch income during the 1930s and 1940s.

In 1952, they worked for a highway contractor out of Mid-west, Wyoming. A year later they applied for their own high-way contract.

Neil's career as a highway contractor would parallel the evolution of the Wyoming Highway Department. The Department (since 1991 known as the Wyoming Depart-ment of Transportation, or WYDOT) was responsible for the transportation infrastructure of the state. Included in its work was the planning and implementation of road build-ing and maintenance. The department awarded contracts through a bid process. On an advertised date and time, the highway department opened competing bids from prequali-fied contractors and awarded the contract in what is known as a "highway letting." Awards went to the lowest bidder. The contractor was held to his "hard bid," or price listed on his bid, which could be changed only under unusual circum-stances and a difficult review process.

Wyoming State Highway Department engineers deter-mined every aspect of highway building including clearing and grubbing, storing the topsoil, excavating, compaction, and surfacing. Additionally, they determined the grade, type of pavement, and details for bridges. Once the bid was award-ed, the contractor worked with State Highway Department engineers at every phase of the project in an ongoing inspec-tion process through final acceptance of the job.

One of Vern and Neil's earliest highway jobs was in the early 1950s, building a road south from Fort Bridger. "I was

Facing page: Neil operating a CAT (Caterpillar) bulldozer on the highway job in 1953 at Birdseye, north of Shoshoni. After the work was complete, heavy rains caused the ends of the pipes to "suck in like tissue paper," according to Neil. Because the bad weather was an act of God, the state paid for the work to be redone. "If they hadn't, I'm not sure we would have made it," says Neil.

working about twenty hours a day," recalls Neil. "I didn't have any help, because I couldn't afford it. I remember this job well because I got to the property line and there was an old rancher standing there with his shotgun. He said, 'you're not crossing here.' I said, 'fella, you are right.'" The county commissioners had forgotten to get an easement on this piece of land. "So we had to back up and go around [his property]."

In 1953, Rissler and McMurry bid on two highway jobs, the Medicine Bow Cutoff and the road between Shoshoni and Thermopolis. Jim Rissler recalls going as a youngster with his father to turn in these two bids. "They didn't expect to get either one," recalls Jim. But they were awarded both at the same time. Panicked, Vern raced home to Casper "to find out where they may have made a mistake on the bid! They were happy to get the work, but scared to death they had left something out and they were going to struggle to make ends meet to complete the job."

"At that time you couldn't pull a bid, as you can today," explains Neil. "If you are awarded a successful bid today, you can pull your other bids." They were stuck with both jobs. "You talk about two scared guys," says Neil. "All that work and no money, and not enough equipment." It was later pub-lished that John Atkins, executive officer of the Wyoming Highway Commission, asked Vern, "Young man, what do you think you're going to do with all that work?" Vern said, "I don't know, sir. Just try to get it done."

Through incredibly hard work and very long hours, Vern and Neil were able to successfully complete both these jobs on time. This was the start of many highways built by Rissler and McMurry across the vast Wyoming prairies and mountains. The company grew quickly. Early on, Vern and Neil developed a division of labor that succeeded through-out their careers. Vern largely took care of the office work,

Neil and Vern building a dam, location unknown. Neil is operating what may be the company's first D7; Vern is standing at right. Rissler and McMurry had just bought the new equipment. "We thought we were really smokin'," says Neil.

though in constant consultation with Neil. Neil spent most of his time on the job sites.

One of the biggest challenges in highway construction is putting together the bid. Vern's brother Harry, who worked for the company for years, explained in a newspaper interview, "most people have no idea how complex the work is. Every line item in a bid must be quoted separately, including materials and labor. The state [Wyoming Highway Department] holds bidders to the unit price, but totals can flex to accommodate unanticipated circumstances." Years later,

Vern explained it much less scientifically. "When Neil and I go out to look at a job, he goes to one side of the hill and I go to the other. We both kick the dirt around and then we get together and guess about what it's going to take to move it."

The Casper newspaper, writing about the company to mark its fiftieth anniversary, reported that "after the company's estimators put together a bid, it wasn't uncommon for Vern to come along and cut the estimates on a lot of items. This practice has earned him the nickname, 'The Butcher.' 'You have to do it,' he says, 'when you need the work, when you're hungry. Taking the work cheap or even at a loss, is better than losing your crew because there isn't any work. You have to take care of your people!'"

Reflecting back on the highway bids, Jim Rissler says, "it was such a risky business because their work was all by contract and you had to turn in bids before you did the work. There was no turning back and no changing the bids. You didn't say, 'Oh, I made a mistake and I can't do it for that.' You had to live with what you bid. It was always fascinating to me how they knew what to bid, especially when they were bidding with new types of equipment and new procedures that they had not tried before." Jim went on to admit that they used to write "WAG" after the bid number they wrote down, standing for "wild ass guess"! Neil McMurry's sons Mick and Vic would later refer to their own contract bidding process as "SWAG," for "scientific wild ass guess," in response to their father's teasing about their college educations.

Rissler and McMurry Company's first big job, between Tunnel Hill and Kemmerer in 1955.

Neil and Vern are long remembered for having many colorful experiences across the state while checking on jobs. For example, one day near Medicine Bow they were driving to the job site bringing parts. "They were always in a hurry to get where they were going," recalls Jim Rissler, who was along on this trip. On that particular day it started raining and Neil's pickup was careening over the prairie "trying to get to some point where we wouldn't get stuck." Finally, they decided to return to Casper, about eighty miles away. By now, the creeks were flooding. Along a dirt road, they came to a bridge over a very full creek. Somebody else was on the other side, as worried about crossing as they were. Vern Rissler walked across the bridge and convinced the other driver to switch vehicles, and they did, enabling each to get

Rissler and McMurry Company operates equipment at a state quarry provided to highway contractors on the I-80 job west of Cheyenne in 1962.

$750,000, recalls Neil. "Vern and I argued half the night over a cent per yard of dirt. Finally, we split it and by doing that we beat W. W. Clyde out of Salt Lake City by $1,500." This particularly pleased Neil. Although he himself occasionally won contracts in surrounding states, he never liked out-of-state contractors getting Wyoming work. "That was our first really big job. We bought some new scrapers, a D9, and a blade. That was when we started to really grow."

For the most part, highway construction in Wyoming is only possible in the summer because Highway Department specifications limit the kind of work that can be done at cold temperatures. As the company grew and took on more employees, Vern and Neil looked for winter employment to help keep their crews together. During the 1950s, the U.S. Government was developing its nuclear energy program. Critical to nuclear energy production is uranium, a mineral found in Wyoming. For two winters, 1957 and 1958, Neil moved his equipment to the Gas Hills to excavate the area for uranium mining. While this helped keep the employees on the payroll, Neil regrets it. "It was very abrasive work and hard on the machinery," recalls Neil. "I think we would have done better if we would have just stayed in highways."

Neil found it increasingly difficult to get to all of his job sites as quickly as he wanted. This was in spite of the fact

home. "Anytime that I went with them, there was always an adventure," says Jim Rissler. Eventually the vehicles were returned to their owners.

Heavy rains also impacted a job in Shoshoni where Neil and Vern built and installed three big eight-foot-high culverts. One night a huge rainstorm twisted the new pipes, requiring them to be removed, damaged sections replaced, then reinstalled.

In late 1955, Rissler and McMurry bid on its next job, the highway between Kemmerer and Tunnel Hill, which was considerably bigger than their previous work. The Wyoming Highway Department estimated the job to be that he has always driven very, very fast. Neil was dubbed "Hurry McMurry" early in his career, particularly for his driving. He has also jumped out of his car to talk with somebody before the car has stopped. "I don't know how many cars I wore out," admits Neil.

Soon after the Kemmerer job Rissler and McMurry was awarded a job in Colorado. "After I got out of the war, I swore that I would never get back in an airplane," claims Neil. "Hell, I really meant it! I had enough of them!" But the distant Colorado job sites posed a recurring problem. "I couldn't drive fast enough on my own, so I started chartering [an airplane] a little bit. It worked so well that I kind of overcame my reluctance to fly. After a while the charter pilots would say, 'Here, you fly and I'll take a nap.'" In 1958, Neil took a few formal flying lessons. In April 1959, he paid seventeen thousand dollars for a brand-new Cessna Skylane 182. "This is a beginner's plane because it is easy to work," Neil says. "You have to really work at it to kill yourself." From then on, Neil flew to most of his far-away job sites. "The fact that I could land out on the road or a dirt strip was beneficial," explains Neil.

The company colors, red and yellow, proved helpful to Neil while he was airborne and navigating to the job sites, because the equipment stood out for miles. Neil and Vern had chosen their company colors to match the equipment brands they purchased. They always used International trucks, which are red, and Caterpillar tractors, which are yellow. After Neil noticed that red and yellow was easy to identify from the air, he had all the equipment painted these colors. Red and yellow, therefore, have always been the official company colors, and Neil's personal favorites.

Neil became well known for his flying. He would carry just about any item to a job site in his plane. "I would load the airplane for Neil," recalls Jim Rissler. "I put the darnedest things into that airplane – brake shoes and truck parts. Neil only got gruff with me once. I had put too many things in one place and he had to re-balance everything in the airplane. I made sure I didn't do it again." The plane also brought payrolls to job sites, making it a welcome sight for construction crews on paydays.

Neil frequently asked his shop manager, Dyce Brownlee, to go along with him in the plane to drop – often literally – parts or payroll. "We had a job near Burgess Junction," Dyce recalls. "It was about 4:30 in the afternoon. Neil said the crusher was broke down and we had the parts they needed. Neil said, 'Why don't you fly up with me and we will just push it [the parts] out of the plane? Why don't you put the payroll in, too?' It was in a box that was wrapped in lots of duct tape. It really crashed when it hit the ground. We were flying and we could see where the guy was sitting out there in the pickup and we started down. I was fighting trying to get the door open and I have this package in my lap. I get the door open and push it out and it stops on the wing! So I'm leaning out and I feel Neil grab me by the back of my pants and finally it falls off the wing, and it stops on the step! Then Neil turned the plane so the package fell off. The guy called and said 'the box just exploded but I got the payroll!' The nuts and bolts scattered and they couldn't find all of them."

Airplane drop-offs became common. They were particularly useful in winters with deep snow. In one winter drop, the trucks were only thirty feet apart, with the drop site between. As Neil's plane dove for the drop, Dyce saw the workers running away. The package landed directly between the vehicles. As Dyce recalls, "When one of the drivers returned he said about that drop, 'My god, I thought it was going to hit the truck and I can imagine at thirty below how I'm going to drive us out of there with a windshield out of it. [The package] just missed the truck.'"

Dyce also remembers a landing in Shirley Basin when Neil flew over some power lines. "I made sure that he still had the wheels up!" says Dyce. There were also several times when Neil flew low to the ground to scare the deer off where he wanted to land. In the Farson area, Neil would sometimes fly his airplane over his relations' places, which included those of his Uncle Vern and three cousins, Jim, Jack, and Bob. Unannounced, Neil would fly over their homes as low as possible "to see if I could wake anybody up," he would say. He would then land on the highway, pull off, and sometimes see if he could get a meal. He never stayed long, though. "Neil was always in a hurry," recalls another cousin and later business partner, Ron McMurry.

Neil often took people in the airplane with him, which usually became a memorable adventure. In 1962, Rissler and McMurry purchased a new airplane. Neil took delivery of the aircraft at Wichita, Kansas, and from there, flew the plane on its maiden voyage to Fort Wayne, Indiana. He was bringing

Facing page: The Rissler and McMurry Company's I-80 project west of Cheyenne in 1962 was the biggest contract awarded by the Wyoming Highway Department up to that time. Vern and Neil were responsible for work on the north side of the interstate, upper left in this photo. This aerial view of the project was taken from Neil's plane.

with him men to drive some new trucks back to Wyoming. Jim Rissler was one of the drivers and accompanied Neil on this night flight. "Neil had no instrument ratings but he had a radio frequency or two that he could use to monitor our location," remembers Jim. "I asked Neil, 'How do you know where the airport is?' He said 'I'm not sure but I think I can get close.' He kept going back and forth on the frequencies, the towns kept multiplying, and finally around 1 a.m. he put the nose down and landed right in Fort Wayne just like he'd done it a million times. Neil could do things like that."

In addition to flying employees for work-related activities, Neil brought Wyoming Highway Department personnel on over-flights to see his highway work from the sky. Neil occasionally took a photographer with him, creating wonderful aerial documentation of construction sites. He often invited youngsters who were at job sites for rides in his plane. "Neil took my six-month-old son Mike and me to Dubois one morning in the plane," recalls Jim Rissler. "Mike slept all the way in the plane through choppy skies. Then we drove in the car to the location, during which time Mike woke up and became sick and upset until we got back to the plane. He slept all through the flight back." Neil usually did not let his adult passengers sleep in his plane, though. He had a reputation for suddenly changing directions to wake up a sleeping passenger!

"One morning we received a call at the office that the Rissler and McMurry Company airplane had crashed not long after takeoff," remembers Jim Rissler, "and that is all we knew. Neil always came home late and left early, and we didn't always know if he was flying or driving. My father was beside himself. I had picked Neil up the night before and thought he said he would be driving. Nothing, though, could ease my father's fears. That morning seemed like an eternity. Finally we were informed that the pilot was from the

When the Rissler and McMurry Company plane crashed in September 1964, everyone worried that Neil had been flying it. The test pilot who had actually flown the plane emerged unharmed.

air service doing follow-up checks on repairs to the plane. We were more than relieved when Neil finally called!" The plane, the same one Neil had flown at night to Fort Wayne, had had technical problems that were never resolved. The pilot, who had flown B-29s during World War II, fortunately was okay. The plane, though, was unsalvageable and had to be replaced by the company's insurance.

In 1959, Rissler and McMurry took its first million-dollar job, on the interstate north of Wheatland in Platte County near a place then known as El Rancho. This was the company's first interstate highway contract. The opportunity arose due to President Dwight D. Eisenhower's decision to improve the nation's infrastructure. His agenda included creating an interstate highway system, which would have a profound impact on the nation, as well as on Rissler and McMurry Company.

The enormity of the project required the company to purchase a new asphalt plant, crusher, two pavers, three rollers, brooms, trucks, and scales. This was a huge investment for a relatively small business, and it required a banker with lot of faith in the company, which Rissler and McMurry had.

Vern and Neil took a few jobs that ended up costing them money. Vern was quoted as saying "The worst job was a project near Afton [the winter of 1959-1960]. We left a lot of money on the table," he said, meaning there had been a large monetary difference between the winning bid and the next higher bid.[2] "The bonding company turned tail and ran, leaving us to endure a forty-five-day wait to get bond." Neil does not have good memories of that Afton job, either. To keep working through the winter, he drilled and dynamited rock to make fill. "I got so sick of snow. While working, if you laid a wrench down, it wouldn't take long and you couldn't find it." The worst part, though, was that Neil and Vern had bid it for dirt work, but the job turned out to be a lot of blasting and drilling, making it considerably more expensive than they had planned.

It happened again at a job in Burgess. Rissler and McMurry submitted a bid anticipating dirt work, but the project turned out to be rock. "That cost us the profits from this job, and another job – the Sunshine Dam at Meeteetse," recalls Neil. There were several challenges in this business that threatened profits. Probably one of the biggest "profit-eaters" was fuel cost. "That could make the difference in profit and loss," explains Neil.

Rissler and McMurry Company moved into even larger-scale highway projects starting in 1962, when it was awarded the contract for a section of new Interstate 80 (I-80) just west of Cheyenne. Neil recalls the company's I-80 bid totaled more than three million dollars, the biggest contract awarded by the Wyoming Highway Department up to that time. It came during a period of increased federal oversight. This was a significant change for Rissler and McMurry, who had started building highways when the industry was still relatively small and the relationship between the contractors and the Wyoming Highway Department was informal. "By the time we had this job with Neil the federal government was cracking down," explains Don Diller, Resident Engineer with the Wyoming Highway Department. Diller had been assigned to oversee Neil's work on the I-80 Cheyenne project. "Everyone was under a lot of pressure," recalls Diller.

The federal crackdown had come as a response to "bid rigging," an illegal business practice in which contractors secretly work together to fix prices on highway jobs, then arrange a system of "taking turns" winning bids. Competing contractors had approached Neil and Vern early on, expecting them to participate in the "bid rigging." Rissler and McMurry Company could have financially benefited from the illegal practice, but Neil and Vern adamantly refused. They insisted they would earn their jobs fairly. This would be their trademark throughout their careers.

A Jersey spreader flattens a windrow of cement treated base on the I-80 job west of Cheyenne in 1962. Rissler and McMurry was the first contractor to use a Jersey spreader with a belly dump on a Wyoming Highway project.

Diller, therefore, did not have to worry about Neil engaging in illegal activities. Rather, the challenges were quite different. "Working for McMurry was an experience," says Diller. "Neil is a pusher. He came in with a lot of equipment and he was on the job all the time. We got along real well with Neil, but it was a lot different than what we were used to. The local contractors were small contractors, but Neil was larger and ran two shifts. He had four or five operations going at the same time on the same job. He moved things around so fast! He just kept us going!"

Diller went on to explain, "We had to do all the surveying and setting the stakes to start the grading, show where the finished grade was for the gravel, and then we had to run all the tests. It was hard to keep up with Neil. We literally worked seven days a week, and sometimes twelve hours a day just to keep up. I didn't see much of my wife and kids that summer. Neither did the other guys with the Wyoming Highway Department. The survey crews, testers, inspectors, and weighmen all had to work seven days a week, two shifts, to keep up with Neil. He was a great guy to work with because he never really had arguments. If he had material out of specification, we just had to tell him and he would fix it." The Wyoming Highway Department employees were not paid overtime for their extra work. They were to be compensated for the extra hours with time off in the winter when work was slow.

Neil finished the two-year job in one year, opening traffic on the new four-lane interstate west of Cheyenne a year earlier than projected. Neil was sitting in a patrol car with Colonel Fred Wickam, Director of the Wyoming State Highway Patrol, when traffic was first allowed on the new interstate. "It was like watching a land rush," remembers Neil. The patrolman claimed the first vehicles were clocked at one hundred miles per hour. "It was great to see. It makes you feel like you did something for civilization." In addition, this particular job "[monetarily] rewarded us well," recalls Neil.

Don Diller would later become the first Director of the Wyoming Department of Transportation.[3] Reflecting back on working with Neil in the early 1960s, he says, "The only people who had trouble with Neil were the people who would not respond to Neil's schedule. I think the ones who had trouble with him were the old-time engineers who were used to a slower pace." Another factor that helped Neil and annoyed some engineers was a change in highway oversight procedures that came in 1956. Prior to this, "1948 specs," or Method Specifications, gave the engineers total control over the contractors' methods. The "1956 specs," called End Result Specifications, required the engineers to measure the end results and complete more documentation. The new specifications allowed the contractor to determine how to do the work, as long as the finished product complied with all specifications and passed the engineers' tests. Neil, of course, figured out the most efficient way to get the job done and comply with specifications. "It was hard for a lot of the older engineers to give up the control they used to have and let the contractor do it the way he wanted to," says Diller.

There was one person, however, who did not think Neil McMurry could get the Cheyenne job done quickly enough. Gus Fleischli owned the truck stop where Neil was working on the connector from I-80 into Cheyenne. The road was obviously torn up for the duration of the project, preventing trucks from getting to the truck stop. "He and I had many, many words about how soon he was going to get it open," recalls Fleischli. Difficulties were resolved over many breakfast meetings, and the two ultimately worked together for decades. Gus also owned Fleischli Oil Company, which sold wholesale lubricants, diesel fuel, and gasoline, primarily to contractors. "We sold Neil McMurry a lot of lubricants and fuels on their contracts," remembers Gus. "Provided we were competitive," he adds. Neil's father had worked for Standard Oil Company all of his life, and Neil felt an allegiance to his father's employer. "He was very loyal to Standard," remembers Gus. "We finally proved to Neil that we had a better product."

Throughout the 1960s and 1970s, Rissler and McMurry Company continued to build hundreds of miles of primary, secondary, and interstate highways all over Wyoming and in some adjacent states. The company built roads near Kemmerer, north of Midwest, ten miles out of Wolcott Junction, and I-25 from Casper to Douglas. They also built sections of I-80 around Laramie, Rawlins, Rock Springs, and the section east of Evanston known as the Three Sisters.

Subcontractors who had been hired to put in the bridges sometimes delayed project completions. By the end of the 1970s "many of the bridge contractors had quit or went

This is the place on the I-80 job west of Cheyenne in 1962 where Neil "almost died of fright." After receiving word that the buried gasoline pipeline here was at a depth of six feet, Neil instructed his crew to dig to three feet and hand-dig the rest of the way. They nearly broke the line at two feet, eleven inches. "Crow Creek would have been on fire, there was gas all the way into Colorado," Neil says. "I shook for days."

At the I-80 job west of Cheyenne in 1962, Neil McMurry and Bruce Emmer work on the Rissler and McMurry Company cement treated base plant. Neil is at center in the lighter-colored shirt.

hot plants (to produce asphalt concrete for paving) and two crushers (to break rock into gravel), with work all over the state. "It was a very capital intensive business," notes Jim Rissler. As the jobs changed, so did the demands on their equipment.

The big jobs also required big crews. The year-round employee numbers fluctuated, of course. Throughout the 1960s and 1970s, a winter work crew could number two hundred, but summer work could require up to three hundred. If jobs were available and someone was willing to give an honest day's work, he or she was hired. Employees were expected to work hard. Superintendent of the Wyoming Highway Department, Leno Menghini, remembers a time back in the 1970s when a young man who had long hair came to Neil asking for a job. Neil looked at him and said, "If you want to work for me the first thing you better do is go and get a haircut." Neil's expectations of his employees were always clear.

Joe Scott noted that when he was growing up in Casper everyone knew of the Rissler and McMurry Company. "Just about every kid in Casper worked for them at some time," Scott claims. The huge crews also required a huge payroll and Neil never missed one. At times this was because his banker was willing to cover it, knowing Neil would repay the bank.

The University of Wyoming Athletic Department approached Neil and Vern about hiring its athletes, particularly in the summer so they could stay in the area. Vern was

broke," explains Neil. "Here I had the whole road paved and couldn't finish it because the bridge wasn't there." In 1981, when Neil would buy Vern out of the business, Neil would also form a bridge division so the company could build its own bridges and have more control over its projects.

To keep up with all the work, Rissler and McMurry expanded its construction assets at various times to two big dirt spreads (the array of equipment used for dirt work), two likely more supportive than Neil of hiring the athletes, who were put to work in the Laramie area. Neil's son Vic remembers an unpleasant experience when Neil, performing one of his unannounced job site visits, caught some of the athletes sitting around. Vic was working with the crew that day and admits they could have been picking up rocks, as they were assigned to do, rather than waiting out a rainstorm. They were also carelessly throwing rocks, and damaged a truck which had recently returned to the field after being repaired in the shop. Neil emphasized to them that they should be working hard and taking care of his equipment.

The Rissler and McMurry children were often included at job sites throughout the summers. "My dad used to throw me in the back seat, with [Neil and Vern] in the front, and I used to get to listen to the two of them carry on. It was always special for me to be with them both," recalls son Jim Rissler. The McMurry family would often accompany Neil in a trailer. Their childhood summer memories are of different places across Wyoming where their dad was working.

As the children grew older, both Vern Rissler and Neil McMurry hired them, as well as other relatives. Pat McMurry, Kenneth McMurry's son and Neil's nephew, started working for the company in 1964 when he was fifteen. "I was still in high school," says Pat. "I swept the floor, then I went to work full-time for them when I graduated, starting as a mechanic." Pat was typical of many in the McMurry family, accepting employment opportunities offered by Neil. "My dad's brother, Harry, was probably with them the longest of anyone," says Jim Rissler. "He was about ten years younger than my father." Jim's two sisters also worked in the office doing secretarial and bookkeeping work. Jim worked for his dad and Neil all through his high school years. "I started when I was around thirteen or fourteen. I swept the shop floors for gas money." Later he operated equipment for the

company part-time until graduating from high school, when he went to work for Rissler and McMurry full-time.

Jim recalls that the rule was no special treatment for the bosses' kids. "Looking back I know that we all got special treatment and attention. The fact that they put us all to work was special treatment in itself. They found a way to include us. They were both patient and considerate enough to look the other way when we did things that only inexperienced kids would do." Jim went on to say that he felt anyone in the family who wanted a job was offered an opportunity to work. "There were times that it cost them money to have us, but they were family-minded enough to include anyone who was capable of working for them, including our sisters, cousins, and in-laws."

Vic recalls, "Dad's rule was that you can work here, as long as you keep your mouth shut, do what you are told by your boss, and I never hear anything about boss's kid syndrome. My sisters worked in the office and Mick and I worked in the shop, cleaning the shop, and cleaning the offices and running parts, and then in the summer we would go out on the jobs. Dad was fierce about that. Dad didn't ever want to hear that his kids were acting like the boss's kids. So we didn't."

Neil McMurry made quite an impression on the many people he worked with while building highways across the state. His unique style was often later noted. For example, Leno Menghini, the last Superintendent and Chief Engineer of the Wyoming State Highway Department prior to its transition to WYDOT, first met Neil when Rissler and McMurry got the contract to do the I-80 section east of Evanston. "I have always appreciated Neil both as an individual and as a contractor," says Leno. "He is a character to say the least. When you sit down with him you have to listen to a few minutes of what I call 'McMurry Speak' or 'McMurryism.' Once you get through that, it's on to business."

The crusher site at Rawlins, 1963. Neil remembers that the wind blew so hard that the 3/4-inch rock was blowing away. "We started crushing nights. We were up on top of that peak drilling, two, three in the morning with the wind really going."

Menghini explains that their conversations would begin with his asking Neil, "How are you doing?" Neil would respond, "Well, I'm going broke because of the engineers for the highway department!" Other times, Neil would insist that his kids had to run around without shoes because he had no money. Then they would discuss the real business at hand. Leno also noted that Neil's organization "was a good one. He was always great to work with." Menghini had a great appreciation for Neil and his work. "Needless to say he was very successful. I attributed that success to Neil always knowing what was going on. He was not an armchair head of an outfit. He was always working, going from job to job."

For those who did not know Neil, his manner of speaking could seem insulting, and was certainly "politically incorrect" to the ears of a later generation, especially when he was referring to someone's ethnic background. For example, Gene "Rocky" Roccabruna was an engineer for the Wyoming Highway Department from Rock Springs when he first met Neil on an I-80 job.[4] The two would meet again near Rawlins on a job out on Separation Flats. Roccabruna claims Neil would call him the "Spaghetti Bender from the Rock Springs Mafia." "I will never forget this one instance," recounts Rocky. "We had all gone to lunch and I had gotten up to go wash my hands or something, and when I got back, there was a plate of spaghetti waiting for me." Later, when working in Cheyenne together, Neil would come into Rocky's office and say, "You got the toughest damn engineers, Roccabruna! Those guys are just beating up on me and no one gives me a break!" Whenever Neil was visiting, Rocky came to expect the lecture.

Neil's jobs around the state brought him opportunities to interact with diverse groups of people. He particularly remembers a lesson he learned while having lunch with Basques on a job on top of the Big Horn Mountains, near

Bridge deck work on Interstate 90 near Sheridan.

Buffalo. The Basques always included wine with their meals. "It's best not to drink the wine until you are ready to leave," explains Neil. An empty glass was always immediately refilled, making it difficult, if one started drinking early in the meal, to get out sober.

Neil's sense of humor is often grounded in sarcasm. "One winter the company was doing a job in Snake River Canyon following a rock slide onto the highway," recalls Jim Rissler. "They had to put a bulldozer up some one hundred and twenty feet above the road to bench the slope and the dozer was right out on the edge of the slope. As the story goes Neil was

Left to right: Bob Miracle, President of the Wyoming National Bank, Vern Rissler, Neil, and Mike Keim, who worked for Caterpillar, stand in front of new equipment purchased by Rissler and McMurry Company in 1972. "We bought a lot of iron from Mike," remarks Neil. H. A. HESS PHOTO

watching from the highway next to a flagman who was stopping traffic when necessary. Someone got out of a stopped car and walked over to Neil to find out if he owned the bulldozer and asked if it made him nervous to see that dozer so close to the edge. Neil looked at him and said no, it didn't. 'The dozer is insured and operators are a dime a dozen.'"

Neil created adventures – and challenges – for others while building his highways. For example, Neil had an asphalt plant located by the Otto interchange about ten miles west of Cheyenne. Nearby he also had a limestone quarry. Running these plants at full production, in an era prior to environmental regulations, created an enormous amount of dust. There are those who claim Neil coated Laramie County with limestone dust one summer! If Neil's blasting caused damage, as it occasionally did, he was quick to repair it to equal or better condition. That was standard operating procedure for Neil.

A rather exciting event occurred at the same limestone quarry in 1963. The United States military had recently placed nuclear missiles near the quarry Neil was using. Neil had drilled in the quarry, and according to Director Don Diller of the Wyoming Highway Department, Neil "didn't like to do a little at a time so he drilled and loaded that thing with dynamite and he set off an enormous shot. I got a call from the commander of the base, stating that all four guys out at that missile base had thought that World War III had started!" In the interest of avoiding a similar mishap, the military invited Mr. Diller and Neil to the missile base for a personal tour. They wanted them to see the sensitive equipment the military had.

Vern and Neil were in the highway business so long that they started to re-do their own work. "Most of the highway designs were for twenty years," notes Jim Rissler, "so after twenty-five to thirty years they would go back and repave roads and add different safety features and design changes." Neil recalls doing sections of I-80 two and three times.

Even though both men employed their children and extended families throughout the years, neither wanted to bring their children in as business partners. Therefore, when Jim had an opportunity to go into business for himself, he left the company. After starting his new business, which included selling dynamite, Jim recalls that "Neil gave me an opportunity to quote him on explosives for a job he was bidding. He had earlier taught me how to use them at the job site, which proved very beneficial with other contractors and miners in the future. He gave me a helping hand when I was struggling with a new business." At the time Jim went into business for himself, there were few suppliers in Wyoming, Montana, or Colorado who sold dynamite and knew how to use it. Jim's knowledge from Neil and his work with Rissler and McMurry Company proved to be invaluable.

Neil shared Vern's approach to sons as partners in the Rissler and McMurry Company. According to Vic, "Dad made it clear early on that we would be able to work in his company until we either quit school or finished school, and then we had to go find something else to do, because he didn't really believe in family businesses. He had seen too many times where the second or third generation took over what the founder had built and didn't understand what work was all about. He often told stories about such companies and how they were on the decline. These were the big contractors when he was starting

Neil McMurry sits in the cab of a new 637D Caterpillar. The equipment is about to leave the yard for a job site.

and they wound up eventually going out of business." Coming home from Vietnam, Mick McMurry would have gone to work for his father, but as Mick explained, "[Neil] just decided that at that particular point in time Vic and I could find our own things to do and so we did." They formed McMurry Brothers Construction Company in April 1970 and soon were in competition with their father and Vern in the highway construction business. The sons' enterprise is described in Chapter 5.

In 1981, after thirty-three years in partnership, Vern Rissler sold his half of the company to Neil. Vern was older and ready to retire, but Neil was not. The Rissler and Mc-Murry partnership had been successful for a variety of reasons. While their personalities were very different, their differences enhanced the business. Even their physical appearances were different, with Vern Rissler standing tall and large-framed, and Neil shorter and thinner. It was not unusual for the two men to argue over almost anything. If there was a genuine disagreement, the two would get in their own pick-ups and go to different job sites. "When we saw each other again, we had moved on," remembers Neil.

The partnership was established and built on decades of mutual trust and respect. Jim recalls his father staying near the phone every evening waiting for the nightly call from Neil checking in with the day's progress. They were in constant consultation with one another and respected one another's opinion. Neil's phone calls continued after the formal partnership ceased, keeping in touch with Vern nearly every day.

"They had a very special relationship," says Jim. In a good-natured manner, "they never agreed on anything. They made sure they didn't. If one said one thing, the other would always say the opposite. One was a Democrat and the other was a Republican. When they couldn't agree on something, they could always talk about politics." Jim continues to hear stories about his father from Neil. "When I was with Neil recently he was commenting on how they got the dozer stuck one day in the Platte River, when I think they only had one dozer. They spent all day getting this dozer out of the river. When [the bulldozer and scraper] were finally loaded and going home they had to go by the Goose Egg restaurant, where they stopped and proceeded to drink a lot and have dinner.[5] After leaving there they were half way up the hill [heading to Casper] from the Goose Egg and my Dad was driving. He

missed a gear in the truck and the bulldozer and scraper all went back down the hill. Neil said, 'You know, your dad could never drive that damn truck!'"

"It was a good partnership," recalls Neil. "I was young and ambitious, while he was older and more prudent." Vern held Neil back while Neil pushed Vern along. "It was a good balance," says Neil. Son Jim Rissler commented that Neil's forward thinking would help his father, particularly when something had not gone well for the company. Rather than mull over the past problem, Neil would insist they move on to the next project. Despite their many differences and occasional disagreements with the business, they had great mutual respect for one another. They always worked out their problems and continued as successful business partners.

Neil and Vern's division of business responsibilities contributed to the company's success. Vern's attention to office responsibilities, including working with bankers and bondsmen, fulfilled a critical side of the business. Neil's hands-on approach to the fieldwork was also important. Neil's unannounced job-site visits immediately perked up employee output. All job sites received frequent visits, assuring the work was getting done, and done well.

After Vern Rissler retired from Rissler and McMurry Company in 1981 at age sixty-seven, he lived an active life for many more years. He went to his office in downtown Casper every day. He served on the Natrona County Commission for eight years, and for twenty-five years was a trustee of Memorial Hospital of Natrona County. He was also a member of the National Defense Committee and served on the Executive Board of the Wyoming National Development Association, Director for the Wyoming National Bank, and Director for the Wyoming Trucking Association, as well as other organizations. Vern was the President of the Wyoming Association of General Contractors in 1973. He received several Casper Area Chamber of Commerce awards. In 1983, he was elected board chairman of Meals On Wheels, an organization he supported for years. Young people benefited from Vern's generosity in numerous ways. He helped build the Casper ball fields, and was often the top bidder at county fair 4-H auctions. Vern would buy animals under his name, Neil's name, and the company's name, all paid for by Rissler and McMurry Company. He would then donate most of the meat to Meals on Wheels.

It is impossible to accurately measure the impact of the Rissler and McMurry Company on the state of Wyoming in general, and on Casper in particular. The *Casper Star-Tribune*, in its 1995 Rissler and McMurry Company Fiftieth Anniversary supplement, listed the company's charitable causes, many of which Vern Rissler was dedicated to: "The City Baseball Diamonds, Casper Speedway, Troopers, 4-H, United Way, and many other projects benefited by Rissler and McMurry's active participation in community affairs." The paper also estimated that Rissler and McMurry Company, during the partnership and under Neil's sole ownership, had funneled 360 million dollars into Casper's economy over the fifty years since the company's founding. Neil's ownership of Rissler and McMurry Company is discussed in Chapter 6.

Rissler and McMurry paychecks also supported thousands of employees over those decades. In some cases, Rissler and McMurry established entire careers for people. Dyce Brownlee admits that when he went to work for Neil and Vern as a young man, he had no direction. "Neil and Vern changed my whole life. I didn't know what I was going to do," admits Dyce. "Then I went to work in their shop and in a few years I was shop foreman. That was what I did the rest of my life, run heavy equipment shops."

Wyoming residents benefited from Rissler and McMurry Company in part because the company had a policy of local

Vern Rissler served eight years as a Natrona County Commissioner. CASPER STAR-TRIBUNE COLLECTION, CASPER COLLEGE WESTERN HISTORY CENTER

purchasing preference, helping other Wyoming businesses. They also benefited because Rissler and McMurry took great pride in its work, giving travelers well-built, safe highways. In addition, the company succeeded through hard work, integrity, and honesty, leaving an example for future generations to admire and aspire to.

CHAPTER 4
NEIL AND ELLIE RAISING A FAMILY

"**After the war I was pretty destitute,**" recalls Neil McMurry. "I used to get seven dollars a month and Ellie got sixty or seventy [while Neil was in the Army]. If she hadn't lived with my folks she would have starved to death, with the baby. When I got out of the service she had no clothes and I had two khaki suits [uniforms] the army gave me. We didn't have a car, didn't have a house, didn't have any blankets, and didn't have any furniture. You could say we were destitute. We weren't at the bottom of the barrel, we were below the barrel."

For those familiar with Neil, this description of his situation immediately after the war is a typical "McMurryism." Ellie was not starving, but rather in the good care of Otto and Alma. She had enough to eat, though due to wartime rationing and modest income, food options were limited. Her closet was likely sparse, again reflective of the time and something she would have been used to, having grown up during the Great Depression on the north side of Casper.

Neil's immediate concern upon returning to Casper was securing employment in order to provide for Ellie, pregnant with their second child, and their baby daughter, Carol, born while Neil was serving in Europe. With his earliest paychecks

Facing page: For their parents' 25th wedding anniversary in 1967, the McMurry children sat for a studio portrait. Left to right: Gayle, Vic, Carol, Mick, and Susan.

Right: Ellie holds her infant son Mick, while nephew Ken McGregor puts his arm around his cousin Carol, 1946.

Ellie at left holds Mick, with Alma holding Carol at right. They stand outside Otto and Alma's house on Melrose Street in Casper, 1946.

from Vern Rissler, Neil was able to purchase a home at 514 South Melrose Street, less than one block from his parents' house. The purchase price for the one-bedroom, one-bathroom, hardwood-floored little house was five thousand dollars. Despite having saved as much as he could from his meager paychecks from Vern, the bank was not impressed with his small down payment. "So I went to Provident Federal Savings and Loan and got a G.I. loan," remembers Neil. Interest on this government loan was very low.[1]

Neil's next concern was to get Ellie an automobile, a rare commodity in the post-war years. Production of cars for civilians had ceased during the war, when the nation's manufacturing efforts were directed exclusively to war machines. "There was a 1939 Hudson that a couple had from California. They were coming through and wrecked it, rolled it over," explains Neil. "So I bought it for a couple of hundred dollars with a stretched out budget." Neil's brother Kenneth worked at a body shop, where the two repaired it. They had to jack up the roof of the car so the doors would work again. They were not able to replace one of the front fenders, so they put a bracket on the car and attached the light to it. "That was my wife's first car," recalls Neil. "She was pretty proud of it." After considerable effort Neil purchased a new pickup for himself. Without a good trade-in, the dealers were not eager to work with him. "I think it was eight hundred dollars in 1947."

Ellie had never driven before, and "I was brave enough to teach her," recalls Neil. "We had Dad's 1934 V-8 stick shift. She forgot to put the clutch in once and we almost went through a building!" The accident was averted, and Ellie learned to drive.

Carol soon had siblings. Neil Albert was born February 5, 1946. He was named for his father, and his middle name likely came from Otto's brother Albert, and Ellie's father, Hugh Albert. Neil Albert's formal name never stuck, and he has always been called "Mickey" or "Mick." Middle child Victor Lee was born April 6, 1947, and is named for Ellie's older brother, Victor, killed in training during World War II. Today, Vic remembers his mother telling him how important it was for her to honor Victor McGregor by giving him a namesake, because he had never lived long enough to have his own family. Gayle Lois, born March 5, 1949, shared her grandmother McMurry's middle name; and youngest child, Susan Anne, was born September 22, 1951.

All the children were born at Memorial Hospital in Casper. Neil was at the hospital when second child Mickey was born. "I had worked all night on the CAT [Caterpillar tractor]," remembers Neil, "and they came and got me in the morning. Ellie was in labor and she had Mickey that night." He missed his second son's birth, though. "I had done all the dams around Casper when Victor was expected, but he didn't come so I went to Lysite to build a big dam for the Pratts [a ranching family]. When I got up there, we got two feet of snow and of course in those days, we were completely paralyzed and I couldn't get home." To get word to Neil about Victor's arrival, the local disc jockey announced it over the radio. It worked. The crew had a portable radio and word got to Neil. Victor was born on Easter and Ellie claimed he was the only Easter lily she ever received. Neil was home for his last two children's births. Susan remembers her mother telling her she was a "holiday baby." Born September 22, Ellie once said, "I thought you figured that out." Susan admitted to not having thought about it!

Even though Neil traveled extensively and for long periods of time for his work, he and Ellie agreed to maintain a permanent home for their children. By the time Gayle, their fourth child, had arrived, the little home at 514 South Melrose Street was quite small. With only one bedroom, Neil recalls putting some of the children in a little sunroom attached to the house. Carol, the eldest, started kindergarten at Jefferson Elementary School while living in this house.

By the early 1950s, when Carol was in the second grade and Susan was a baby, the family moved to a bigger home at 1452 Bonnie Brae Street. This was a modest house with two bedrooms downstairs and an apartment built over the garage, where the boys stayed. "We were just like our neighbors, except our dad didn't come home every night," recalls Carol. Their new home was across the street from Grant Elementary School, which all five McMurry children attended. There are memories of the teachers parking in front of the McMurry picket fence and spontaneous parent-teacher conferences taking place.

Neil's work pattern was soon established. It consisted of long days, usually seven days a week, and frequent trips away from Casper. Ellie was raising the children with help from her parents, Hugh and Stella McGregor, and Neil's folks, Otto and Alma McMurry. All the grandparents were relatively young when Neil and Ellie started their family. When their first child Carol was born, Otto was only forty-four years old and Alma was a year younger. Ellie's father, Hugh, was the oldest of the grandparents, fifty-two at Carol's birth, and his wife, Stella, was forty-six years old.

The McMurry grandparents' involvement with Neil's young family had begun during the war when Ellie stayed with them while Neil was overseas. Otto and Alma had no daughters, and welcomed the chance to have a young woman in their home. "It didn't hurt that she gave them their first grandchild, too," admits Neil. "My parents adored Carol. She was real cute, with her big brown eyes." Otto would take Carol down to the local pub and have a drink and show her off. "People used to ask whose little girl are you, and she would say, 'Daddy's girl!'" recalls Neil. Carol would have a special relationship with these grandparents throughout her childhood.

Neil and Ellie's children would often take turns spending the night at their McMurry grandparents' home, the same house where their father had been raised, at 424 South

Caspers's Center Street in 1947. TOM CARRIGEN PHOTO, COURTESY WYOMING STATE ARCHIVES, DEPARTMENT OF STATE PARKS AND CULTURAL RESOURCES; HOLT-GRAY COLLECTION, CASPER COLLEGE WESTERN HISTORY CENTER

only did they have to compete with their siblings to be the only child to stay with Alma, but often with cousins, too, who were given the same opportunity. "I just always wanted to be there," recalls Vic. "She told a lot of stories, she talked a lot. I have fond memories of falling asleep with my grandmother talking."

Ellie could depend on Otto and Alma for more than help with her children. If something needed to be done while Neil was away, Otto would do it. "Otto was the handyman for Ellie all the time," recalls Mick.

There were times, though, when Otto's antics could be a bit stressful for Ellie. While out on a fishing trip at a place called Cunningham Corral in the foothills of the Big Horns, Otto may have enjoyed too many Coors beers and wound up bringing home a "bum," an orphaned lamb, for his grandchildren. Otto hooked the lamb to Ellie's clothes-line. Vic remembers his mother saying, "Otto McMurry, if I can ever catch up with you I'm going to kill you!" Ellie's little kids, not surprisingly, were fond of the lamb. Ellie eventually won out, though, and the lamb was removed from her backyard. Undaunted, Otto brought two or three ducks for Ellie and his grandchildren one Easter. The duck droppings made the backyard a smelly mess, and again, Ellie had the "pets," or rather "pests," removed.

Melrose Street. The house was big to the little children, especially with a basement. "I remember spending a lot of time at their house. Otto was a lot of fun," recalls Carol. Susan remembers it much the same. "We spent a lot of time with Grandpa Otto and Grandma Alma. We used to take turns spending the night over there. Grandma always had these popcorn poppers." Mick remembers the dark green canvas tent Otto set up in his backyard for them to camp in. "It was almost like winning the lottery, getting to go spend the night with Alma, especially when Otto worked the graveyard shift," so that he had his grandmother to himself, remembers Vic. Not

Otto usually drove Alma and some of the grandchildren to the public library every Saturday. "He would drop us at the library and he probably went and had a beer," laughs Susan.

"I think that is where we got our love for reading, because Grandma took us to the library and we would get a week's supply of books." The Casper library at this time, built as a replica of Jefferson's Monticello, had closed stacks. That is, only the librarian had access to the shelves of books. Alma was a good friend of the librarian, who allowed Alma and the grandkids to go into the stacks, which was a big deal. Alma was an avid reader. Everyone remembers Alma with a book.

Otto enjoyed working in his garden. "He was a nervous-type person," explains Neil. "He only worked forty hours a week at the refinery" and had a lot of energy left over, much of which was spent on his big garden. "He was always trimming trees," adds Neil. "I remember Mother trying to stop him [because] when he got through there was only a stick!" "He had a great garden," confirms Susan. "He had a big cherry tree in the middle of it and tied pie tins to it to keep the robins out of it. He really had a green thumb." Mick remembers the big tomatoes and onions Otto grew and consumed raw directly from the garden.

Grandpa Otto seems to be remembered most, however, for his fishing. He retired from Standard Oil Company in 1959 while his grandchildren were still young and all at home. "He always used to take the boys and me fishing," says Carol. Younger sister Susan remembers fishing with Otto, too. Vic claims his lifelong love of fishing was in part nurtured by Otto. "Growing up I have wonderful memories of going camping and fishing in the Big Horn Mountains with Otto. Sometimes my grandmother would go, and other times it was just Otto and me," reminisces Vic. A deep bond was developed between Otto and his grandchildren during their fishing trips. "He was a wonderful man," Vic continues. "I have great respect for him. He had such integrity and honesty. He was such a pleasant man, such a joy to be around. You always knew where Otto stood."

Ellie holding Gayle, with Mick at left and Vic at right, at their home, 514 South Melrose Street.

Neil and Ellie's children spent time with Ellie's folks, too. Hugh, called "Huey," played the fiddle, and with his red nose and Scotch whiskey, he seemed the stereotypical Scotsman. "He would take a drink out of his whisky bottle and make a face like he was in great pain, then he'd do it again," remembers Neil. Carol recalls him "sitting around and smoking his pipe. He was very quiet." A mechanic, he would often help Ellie with her car when Neil was away. Huey had a heart attack in the mid-1950s when he was in his sixties. He survived, but was compelled to retire.

The McGregor grandparents had little money. They lived in north Casper, a poor section of town. The simple home was heated with a coal-burning potbelly stove. A yellowish tint stained the interior walls, residue of the coal. Huey and Stella would hang plastic over the windows in the wintertime in an effort to keep the heat in and the cold out. In later years, a space heater helped. The McGregor's little home made the McMurry house appear much bigger.

Carol used to enjoy going to the McGregor house on Friday evenings because it was near the roller skating rink. Mick recalls the grocery store next door, with its stucco exterior and wooden floor. On a special occasion, they got a fudgesicle there.

Stella was very different from Huey. "She was shrill, very excitable," remembers Carol. Susan recalls her as very strict. "Grandma Stella used to baby-sit us and she ran a really tight ship," says Susan. One time Huey and Stella were staying with the McMurry children while Neil and Ellie were away. Huey had spent the day at the Eagles Building, while Stella was home with the kids. Carol became ill with scarlet fever, and her condition worsened throughout the day. Stella was unable to take Carol to the doctor, because she did not drive. Upon Huey's return, he sat on the couch, unconcerned. Stella, on the other hand, was frantic. "Huey!" Stella yelled, "this child is going to die! How are we going to tell Neil and Ellie when they come home? She's going to die!" The doctor made a house call, and Carol recovered.

Neil's fast driving also induced Stella's excitability. It was common on a family outing for all the children to sit in the back seat of Neil's big car, with Neil driving, Ellie next to him, and Stella by the window. "Elnora!" Stella would yell, "tell Neil to slow down! He's going to kill all these babies!"

Stella is also remembered as an accomplished seamstress. "She could sew and crochet anything," recollects Susan. "She was very talented." Carol remembers a beautiful silk suit Stella made for her when she married. Stella never purchased patterns, but rather made her own out of newspaper.

Ellie's youngest sibling, brother Richard, and his wife, Ellen, never had children of their own and spent a lot of time with Ellie's family. Vic recalls as a child attending Dick and Ellen's wedding. At the point in the ceremony when it was asked if anyone present had any reason to dispute the marriage, Vic considered speaking up. He did not want Uncle Dick to get married, and become too busy for him. Apparently it was not a problem; Dick and Ellen continued to include Vic in their lives. Vic remembers as a young adolescent running away from home and going to Uncle Dick and Aunt Ellen's house. "I remember being really distraught a few times, so I ran away on my bicycle and went to their house."

When Vic was a young man, he and Dick would spend a lot of time together attending high school football games, fishing, and listening to country music. The two were known to stay up nights recording 45 rpm records onto cassette tapes for Vic to listen to in his car's cassette player as he drove around the state for his work. Dick, an accountant, had the Hat Six Creek Ranch on the east side of Casper as a client. Through this connection, Dick and Vic were able to camp and fish on the property.

Although Neil was gone from Casper much of the time, especially during the summer, he kept in touch with Ellie and the children. During the school year, the children were home with Ellie, but on Sundays they would often come visit Neil on job sites. "She would bring the kids and a case of beer," recalls Neil.

Ellie had loved her first car, the restored wreck of a 1939 Hudson, but she liked her very first new Lincoln, in 1952, even better. In the photo at left, she stands in front of that vehicle parked at an early Rissler and McMurry highway job south of Fort Bridger. The converted city bus in the background was living quarters at the site. Ellie always enjoyed having her own car.

If Ellie was not spending a Sunday taking the kids to a job site, she would often take them to Sunday School at the Methodist Church, though she did not attend with them. Neil's parents had never attended church, and while Ellie's parents were Catholic, only Stella attended church regularly. Neil and Ellie had chosen not to marry in the Catholic Church, which had resulted in Ellie's excommunication. On top of that, the priest who had officiated her brother Victor's wartime funeral made it clear to Ellie, pregnant at the time, that her marriage outside the church had made her unborn child a bastard. These bitter experiences turned Ellie against the Church, and she would never return, despite visits from Catholic priests during her final illness.

Occasionally Neil would let Ellie know he was coming home for an evening, and Ellie would always delay dinner with the family until his arrival. "Then something would go wrong on the job and we would be hungry," recalls Carol. Ellie would insist on waiting even as late as 9 p.m. Once home, Neil often entertained the children. When they were little, he would walk up and down the stairs – on his hands! The keys and change would fall from his pockets as he showed off his strength to his kids. Susan remembers her dad lying on his back and lifting her up as she stood in his hands. Neil recalls doing the same with Gayle.

During the summers Ellie would load the children in her latest Lincoln and go to stay at Neil's job site. They would

Ellie and Neil, far left, at their "home away from home" near Kemmerer in May 1957. Next to Neil is his old friend from the war, Raymond McMillan, wife Ruby, and their children. At far right are Ellie's sisters Mary Lou and Francis, with their children.

just be with Dad," says Susan. "We were going to be a family."

They traveled all over the state, from Ham's Fork outside Kemmerer, to Medicine Bow north of Laramie, while Neil built the highways around these towns. Their favorite summers may have been the ones spent at Hale's Silver Stream Lodge in Afton on the western edge of the state, where Neil rented a house for the family. Another time, the family joined Neil south of Waltman, Wyoming, where he was enlarging a ranch dam. It was late in the year and what little water was left in the dam froze. The kids brought their ice skates and used the frozen reservoir as a rink.

In the summer of 1955, the family camped near Lake Viva Naughton on a bend of the Ham's Fork near Kemmerer. The children persuaded Neil's cousins, Jim and Bob McMurry, who were working for Neil that summer, to help them build a raft. It was not a difficult task because the area ranch had scrap railroad ties and wood scattered throughout. With the aid of the older cousins, Mick and Vic began building the watercraft. Ellie heard about the project and insisted it stop, fearing for her children's safety. Ignoring their mother, the raft was completed and the McMurry children and cousins piled on for a ride. When the overloaded raft came around the bend in the river next to where the yellow trailer was parked, Ellie was watching just as it broke up, scattering logs, railroad ties, and

stay in Neil's trailer, with all five children sleeping in the bed while Neil and Ellie had the couch. The yellow house trailer did not have a refrigerator or electricity, but it did have mice in the walls. When possible they parked near water, giving the children a great place to play and fish. Other times they had to camp in the middle of a desert. The family often ate antelope Neil had shot off the prairie and in cooler weather, stored on top of the trailer to save the meat from other animals. "I think that was important for us, to children across the river. "Jimmy Crack Corn!" yelled Ellie, referring to Jim McMurry by his nickname after a popular song at the time, "If I catch you, I'm going to kill you!" With lots of laughs and shouts, everyone made it safely to shore.

Riding on their dad's construction equipment at the job sites was always fun for Neil's children, and at young ages, Mick and Vic started driving the tractors. The boys' first paid employment, though, was painting the guardrail on a job near Kemmerer. It was in the mid-1950s and Vic and Mick were about nine and ten years old. "I paid them fifty cents a day plus board and room," recalls Neil. Ellie was not pleased that Neil had her sons out working in the full sun on this job without sunglasses, and reminded him of this for years to come.

Mick and Vic do recall this employment, but not surprisingly, they have more pleasant memories of fishing and arrowhead hunting at their dad's job sites. Arrowhead hunting could be particularly lucrative after the scraper moved untouched ground. Collecting rocks was also common. "They were stripping one of the first open pit uranium mines at the Gas Hills in 1957," remembers Mick. "We would go out on weekends when they were doing maintenance on the equipment and dig up the uranium ore and bring pieces home. We put them in our bedroom and my mother would complain about them, so we used to hide them under our beds." Uranium ore is a crumbly sandstone, leaving a mess wherever the boys put it.

In another adventure, this one in 1959, Neil's company was clearing a rockslide in the Snake River Canyon for traffic to get through and to make room on the mountain in the event of another slide. Neil himself was working on a job in Thayne, when he decided to check on the work being done in the slide area. Taking along a few of his children, "he ran down there – at one hundred miles per hour!" claims Vic,

who was with his dad on this trip. The bulldozer was working a few hundred feet above the highway, pushing gravel and dirt off the hillside. The operator would not have been able to see down to the road. Neil, wanting to talk with the operator, had his flaggers hold traffic on both sides. With a good running start, he drove up the hillside of loose gravel and dirt. The two-wheel-drive car bounced and jumped until it made it to the top. On this particular day, the bulldozer operator was ready to push off a load of dirt when he saw Neil just in time. "Dad admitted it was a close call," recalls Vic. Neil did not always make it to the top on similar stunts, sliding down sideways, then trying it again. He never did roll a vehicle driving up the steep, loose dirt hillsides to check on his operators, despite the many times he did this.

Neil's children also had many experiences with him in his airplane when visiting job sites. One of their favorite stunts in both the car and the plane was when Neil would "tickle their tummies!" When driving up a steep hill, Neil would really accelerate, then let off the gas at the top, giving his little passengers a tickle in their tummies. Neil could produce the same effect in his airplane by quickly pulling it up and dropping it down. He was known to pull this trick on sleeping passengers, and the effect on their stomachs woke them up.

On the flying trips the children also learned about "sucker holes," or openings in the clouds during storms, when visibility was getting poor. Sometimes Neil would use these holes in the clouds to get above the weather. Neil always flew visually, without instruments, so he became very good at learning the conditions of the sky. Occasionally, though, sucker holes were not available and the weather was poor enough that Neil needed to land his plane. This happened once near Independence Rock when son Vic was with him. Vic was eager to go arrowhead hunting as soon as Neil's plane had landed on the highway. Vic was never concerned

Neil would land his airplane on the highway he was constructing.

for his own safety during these flights with his father piloting the airplane.

Sometimes on Saturdays the family would go to the closest town to stock up on groceries and get ice cream. Mom and Dad would get "adult time" enjoying a drink in the local bar, while the kids hung around outside. This was common in Wyoming throughout the 1950s and 1960s, when the towns were small and safe. After a shopping trip to town, the kids would often get soda pop, and Ellie would line up five glasses to ensure everyone got the same amount. The baby of the family, Susan, does not remember it as always equitable. "I was the youngest so I never got any of it!"

Some weekends, during good weather, the family would

make a "mad dash" to Salt Lake City or Denver, recalls Mick. "We would pick up parts or supplies, and hopefully have enough time to see a movie, have dinner, then it was back to the field."

When Carol was a little older, Neil would take her along on extended driving trips to help keep him awake. They would talk a lot with each other while he moved equipment or made a delivery. "I loved these trips because he let me eat all the junk food I wanted. It was hot in the summer time and we would get pints of ice cream, or candy, or a Coke." Carol also recalls learning to drive on the Wyoming prairies with her father. "At age twelve I drove from the Farson Cutoff to Casper and I knew how to drive when I got home. I remember he gave me this lecture about how not to ride the clutch. He said, 'there is a little thing in there that does not cost much, called the throw out bearing. If you ride the clutch and it goes out, it will cost one hundred dollars to repair it. So, don't ride the clutch.'"

During the mid-1950s, when Neil was working near Kemmerer, he wanted to purchase additional equipment. He worked with a dealer in Idaho who had secured work for Neil with the new equipment on the new railroad grade into Atomic City. While working there, Neil purchased a Zenith Oceanic Radio. "It was a big black thing. You would open it up at the top where it had an antenna. You could pick up radio stations from all over the world," remembers Carol. "Mick, Vic, and I would stay up late at night and listen to this." Vic recalls listening to it in the trailer in Atomic City, and hearing Elvis Presley for the first time. Carol's memory of that radio and those times were when she heard Marty Robbins singing "A White Sport Coat and a Pink Carnation." The radio followed the family in their subsequent homes.

Mick McMurry, age 7, "driving" a D8 Caterpillar with a sheep's foot roller at a job site north of Medicine Bow in 1953. This equipment compacts earth.

It took a lot more effort for the family to get a television, which Ellie very much wanted. In Casper during the 1950s and 1960s, television required a cable hook up in addition to the set. Both of these were expensive. "My mother would tell us to talk up the TV when Dad came home," remembers Carol. "Dad would say, 'we're not getting a goddamn television.'"

Vern Rissler, on the other hand, liked to get the latest things. The Risslers got a television early. "We would go over there every Saturday night so we could watch the Disneyland channel," remembers Carol. "All seven of us would go. I think Vern finally told Dad to get his own TV! It wasn't that Neil didn't want to spend the money, but he thought televisions were frivolous." Susan has similar memories. "We had to beg Dad for a television." Neil recalls the problem as being expense. "I didn't have the money – it was $300, $400, or $500 just for the hook up! The kids cried and cried until finally I gave in." "When we finally got it, it was a huge box with a little, tiny screen," recalls Susan. "We could only watch it for half an hour a day, so we had to choose between Mickey Mouse, Howdy Doody, Lone Ranger, or Rin Tin Tin` after school. But on Friday nights we got to watch the fights when Dad was home."

Vic has a vivid memory of how the family television impacted his childhood. One day Vic decided to take a quick ride on his bike during his school lunch break, but unfortunately fell off the sidewalk and hit his temple on the curb, receiving a concussion. His recovery required a fortuitous two-week stay at home, coinciding with the 1955 World Series. It was the first year the Brooklyn Dodgers won, and Vic was able to watch on the family's new television set, thanks to his injury. He became a big fan of the Brooklyn Dodgers, and set out to play baseball himself. The following summer he started his Little League career. It lasted for a couple of years, but without a lot of support from his father. "What the hell are you doing wasting your time doing that, when you could be out here on the job working with me?!" barked Neil.

Vic's baseball training resulted in at least one memorable experience. Again home from school during lunch break, Vic was in the backyard hitting marbles with his baseball bat. In his young imagination, the backyard was really Ebbets Field, home of the Brooklyn Dodgers. He tried hard to get the marbles, or baseballs, over the hedge like the professionals. When the school bell rang, the game was over, and Vic returned to school. Somehow, he did not notice that the car in front of his home had a shattered driver's side window. The driver, convinced he had been shot at, had called the police. Vic was completely surprised when the policeman and his mother found him at school later that afternoon. Ellie had deduced that her son's marbles had caused the accident. "Vic had a knack for getting in trouble," Ellie would claim.

While Vic was working on his baseball career, Gayle was distinguishing herself as a baton twirler. Her instructor was Lynne Vincent, who would later be Lynne Cheney, the U.S. Vice President's wife. Gayle's best friend, Linda Pouttu, remembers traveling with Gayle and watching her compete in costumes made by Grandma Stella McGregor. Gayle would often bring home first or second place awards. Neil recalls watching his daughter on live television in a baton-tossing contest, which she won. Announcing the award was a local businessman, simultaneously promoting himself and his meat products. Gayle was handed a package of hotdogs as her prize. "Gayle said, 'My mother doesn't allow us to eat those wieners!' right on live television!" laughs Neil. "She didn't care!"

Ellie was busy raising five children mostly by herself, yet she found time to be active with her children's activities and in the community. She worked as a Boy and Girl Scout leader and served as "room mother" for the children's classes.

Ellie also volunteered for "The Casper Project – An Enforced Mass-Culture Streptococcic Control Program" with Dr. Robert Fowler, a program in the Casper schools to test children for strep throat, caused by streptococcic bacteria. The program tested for and treated other infections as well. Mick contracted rheumatic fever, a complication of strep throat, when he was very young, giving Ellie personal interest in the cause. In 1958, *The Journal of the American Medical Association* featured an article about this work in Casper.[2]

Reflecting back on their childhoods, the McMurry children have many fond memories. "I had a great childhood,"

Vic McMurry's 1959 Little League team, with coach Mr. Scott at far right. Vic is second from left. Neil thought Vic should be working with him, instead of playing baseball, but Vic played Little League for a few years nonetheless.

declares Mick. "Life in Casper was simple. We didn't have a lot but we didn't know that." Mick adds that they spent a lot of time with extended family, including grandparents, aunts, uncles, and cousins. Vic says, "I had a wonderful childhood. I felt really grounded. We knew what the rules were, we didn't see Dad a lot in those early days, but it wasn't like we felt his absence. Mom and Dad had a system worked out that he was kind of the enforcer, and she spent all the time with us. Mother was a wonderful woman. She was a loving mother."

Friends of the McMurry children have similar memories of growing up in Casper with them. Childhood friend Bucky Walker, who went to school with Mick from kindergarten through college, remembers their childhood fondly. "For entertainment we played baseball, road our bicycles every-where, and found our own entertainment. We played 'Kick the Can' and 'Mother May I?' and 'Hide and Seek.' I think we had a very healthy, simple, wonderful childhood." Occasion-ally Neil would drive home a big truck and lowboy trailer usu-ally covered with mud. While parked in front of the Bonnie Brae home, the boys would have great fun throwing the mud at one another and at other targets in the neighborhood.

Extended family was important to the McMurrys and McGregors. Alma particularly enjoyed her relationships with her daughters-in-law. Betty McMurry was married to Neil's brother Don, a career U.S. Army officer. Early in their marriage she was not able to go overseas with her husband, so she spent a lot of time with his mother. "We used to sit out on the front porch on the glider and drink beer and smoke cigarettes," recalls Betty. "Alma would tell one story after another. I really liked her a lot. Alma was really good to me." Betty also remembers Alma telling her that the happiest time in her life was raising her boys. After her children were grown, though, Alma wanted to work at the library, but Otto would not let her, which was typical of working men in the

post-World War II years. So she filled her time with family, books, and often a few drinks.

Later, Don was able to bring his wife and young family overseas, giving their six children the experience of living in another country. This meant they were not in Casper as much as were their cousins, and therefore did not have the opportunity to get to spend a lot of time with Alma. One time, when the family was home on furlough between Don's assignments, Alma said to them, "You know, one of us isn't going to be here when you get back." The day after they arrived on his next tour of duty in Turkey, on August 1, 1960, Alma suffered a stroke and died. According to a newspaper account she died suddenly and had not been in ill health.[3]

Alma was loved and missed by everyone in her family. The children of Neil's brother Kenneth, who lived in Casper, especially missed their grandmother after her active partici-pation in their young lives. Neil and Ellie's children did, too.

Life changed for the McMurry family in 1962, when Neil completed the Cheyenne highway job. The financial success of this project resulted in the family building a new, bigger home at 1455 South Ash Street, not far from Dean Morgan Junior High School and Natrona County High School, which all the children attended. Some of the topsoil from the Chey-enne job was used in the yard in Casper. Susan, the young-est child, left Grant School to finish her grade school at Park School near their new home.

When Susan was in junior high school, Ellie started vol-unteer work in the Casper Daycare Center at the Presbyte-rian Church, the same church in which Ellie and Neil had married. This was the start of Ellie's nearly two-decade commitment to the Center and its children. The preschool was established for mentally challenged and developmen-tally delayed children, and continues in this capacity today. The children there called her "Aunt Ellie." Susan also worked

Neil, Otto, Don and Ken McMurry in the 1960s, standing outside the house at 1455 South Ash, built in 1962.

at the Daycare Center occasionally. This work with children brought Ellie great pleasure and fulfillment.

By the time both sons were in high school, they worked full-time for Rissler and McMurry Company during the summers and part-time during the school year. Wyoming Highway Department engineer Don Diller oversaw Neil's I-80 job west of Cheyenne in 1962, and remembers Mick and Vic. "Both boys were on that job," recalls Diller. "I don't think they were old enough to operate the equipment but they did. I know Mick ran a roller and Vic did a lot of the parts chasing for the mechanics." All the daughters also started at a young age working for their dad's company, in the office. On their dad's

The McMurry family in the late 1950s. **Back row, left to right:** Pat and Ken McMurry, Otto, Carol, Ellie and Neil. **Middle:** Ken's sons Mark, Kent and Patrick; Mick standing at center. **Kneeling:** Vic, Gayle and Susan.

As previously noted, in the summer of 1962, Vic worked for his dad driving parts for the company on the I-80 construction job east of Cheyenne. Fifteen at the time, he had recently gotten his full driver's license. Vic brags, "I used to tell my friends, 'Can you believe this? I get paid two dollars an hour and all I do is drive. They give me a vehicle, buy the gas, and I drive all day long.'"

Mick and Vic also worked with Neil the next summer in Rawlins. On these summer jobs, Neil rented housing for his sons. The young men had the opportunity to meet and work with many other interesting Rissler and McMurry employees. These older men accepted the boss's children, a consideration Vic and Mick appreciated. "They were good people," remembers Vic of his older co-workers during his youthful summers working with them. "They were dedicated to Rissler and McMurry. I admired them when I was young, and I admire them even more now."

With their wages, the young McMurry boys had been able to purchase vehicles. By age thirteen, Mick had a Cushman Super Eagle motorcycle, which he used to transport himself to and from school everyday, often with Vic on the back seat. Soon Mick graduated to a car and Vic purchased the motorcycle from Mick. Vic promptly crashed it, injuring his foot and leg and putting himself on crutches for ninth grade. At age fifteen, Vic purchased a used 1955 Ford from the neighbors. "I had the only car that I was aware of at Natrona County High School that I could play 45 rpm records in!" boasts Vic. He purchased a Norelco record player from J. C. Whitney, a mail-order auto-parts house. Mechanics at the Rissler and McMurry shop mounted the record player under the dash for him. "It was great for pick-ups!" Vic claims. Thanks to a local juke box company, Vic was able to purchase the latest Rolling Stones and Beatles songs in Casper. Not long afterward, Vic traded in his "Rock and Roll" Ford for a

highway jobs, Gayle and Susan also "flagged," or directed traffic through the construction sites. Neil recalls one time a man ran through Susan's stop sign and she responded by hitting his car with her sign. He immediately stopped, went over to a car parked close to Susan, and started kicking it. "It's not my car," said Susan, "so I don't care if you hurt it!" In exasperation, the man left. Gayle got in trouble while working as a flagger for attending to her suntanning and not paying enough attention to traffic. Better yet were the times she held back a carload of young men to socialize with, rather than keeping the traffic moving.

new 1963 Dodge Dart Swinger with the latest in automotive technology: a push-button gearshift on the dashboard and bucket seats.

Despite Neil's long absences from home while he worked, his presence was always felt. Ellie compiled a report card of sorts for Neil, detailing bad behavior by the children. "Carol and Mick were never on it," recalls Vic, "but Gayle and I were on it a lot, and sometimes Susan." Mick admits that he often attended the same beer parties as Vic, but always seemed to escape before being caught by parents or sometimes the police. Vic, however, seemed to always get in trouble. "It was probably because he had the long hair," suggests Mick.

Vic recalls that when he got into trouble during high school, the episodes often included Ellie's perpetual support, combined with his father's punishments. Vic always paid for any damage he caused, such as the repairs to the school superintendent's car after he hit it. Once, Neil even punished him with a haircut! Still, Vic enjoyed his high school years. "I loved my growing up years. I still look back thinking those were great times. We had this family nucleus. I knew who my parents were and I was comfortable that they were very solid parents. They really did love each other, and had supportive family around them."

Again, the children's friends share good memories of Ellie. "I was always very envious of the McMurry kids because they had such a great family home," recalls Mick's lifetime friend, Bucky Walker. "It was always a very nice home and I loved Ellie. I absolutely adored her. She was like a second Mom to me. She was just so loving, caring, and interested in our lives, in who we were. She was just a very solid woman. She was never condescending, always gave good advice, and she made sense. She ran a pretty tight ship." Ellie did not have her mother's excitability, though many remember her as feisty.

Mick and Vic were teenagers working at Neil's job site near Rawlins in 1963 when the boys discovered this cartoon in the July *Mad Magazine*. They stayed up late to present the cartoon to Neil when he returned from work. Neil has kept the clipping in his desk drawer ever since.

Ellie is remembered by family and friends as an excellent cook and homemaker.

Gayle's lifetime friend Linda Pouttu has similar memories of her friend's mother. "Ellie was such a warm-hearted, kind, and sweet woman," recalls Linda. "She was just love and kindness. She was an excellent cook. Everything she made was excellent. There were always things around that she had made. Their house was always spotless. She had all the teenage boys trained to take their shoes off at

the door. When you came in the foyer of their house, there would be heaps of dirty tennis shoes. She raised respectful gentlemen."

The McMurry children's friends also share similar memories of Neil. "I always looked up to Neil," remembers Linda Pouttu. "He was an inspiring man. He wasn't home very much, but when he came in, he was so suave. He had his fedora hat. He was charming – a real gentleman. I respected him so much. He worked so hard, had such a nice family, and I liked all of them. He was always someone I wanted to acknowledge." Carol's high school friends, too, used to comment to her about how handsome her father was.

Bucky Walker remembers they were on their best behavior when Neil was around. "That's because he would tell us if we weren't!" says Bucky. "He was always up front, teasing a lot but a lot of times when we were at that age we didn't take it as being teased. I would have never done anything to make him intentionally mad. He was always so good to us, too, when we were growing up. He was always kind and fair. The first time I rode in a brand new car it was his car. The first time I ever flew in a private airplane it was his plane. He was very good about sharing what he had with kids like me who had nothing."

All five of Neil and Ellie's children graduated from Natrona County High School, like their parents had. Carol graduated in 1962, and by her own admission, was a studious kid. "I was kind of a nerd," affirms Carol. "I was the president of the Latin Club for four years while taking Latin." She remembers getting good grades in all her subjects except math. They all wore uniforms. For the girls it consisted of a navy blue or black skirt, white blouse, and navy blue or black sweater, "provided your collar was out, proving you were wearing something under your sweater!" adds Carol. Economically, the McMurry family was in the middle. "There were families with less money than us and those with more and they usually wore the Jantzen sweaters," says Carol. In the 1960s, Jantzen sweaters were a high-quality and relatively expensive brand found at Kassis Department Store in downtown Casper. "We couldn't always get a new pair of shoes, but neither could many of our classmates," Carol adds.

When not in class or studying, Mick spent his time working for his dad. He graduated in 1964. Brother Vic, who graduated a year later, had used his high school extracurricular time differently. Both sons brought home good grades, but Vic seemed more interested in his social life than what was going on in class or at work. Juggling this conflict became problematic for Vic. "Mick and I were working the shop in the winter and if a piece of equipment broke down on a Friday afternoon and they needed it on Monday or Tuesday, they would haul it in and the first thing we had to do was steam clean it. So that would be our Friday night job and then the mechanic worked Saturday and Sunday fixing it. I can remember sometimes feeling sorry for myself, knowing my friends were out and I'm steaming a loader or dozer," Vic recounts.

A big part of Vic's high school career was playing in the band, "The Eddies." "I didn't have any music training and I really never could play, and I damn sure couldn't sing." When Vic was a sophomore, his friend Don Teasdale had taken him to see Corey McDaniels and Paul Huber, who were practicing and trying to form a band. One guy was playing the guitar, another was working the organ, and the third was on the drums. "They said 'we need a bass player,'" recalls Vic. Though Vic admitted to having no experience, they handed him a bass guitar and showed him how to play the only four notes in the hit song 'Louie, Louie.' "I was immediately hooked," says Vic.

The Eddies were a big success. The band's name came from Vic. One of the times he was caught in school not doing what he was supposed to be doing, the teacher asked him, "What is your name?" "Eddie," Vic replied, and the name stuck and worked well for the band name, too. They played regularly for dances at the Industrial Building on the Casper Fair Grounds. One summer Vic did not go to the field to work, but rather stayed in Casper and worked in the shop and played in the band.

Neil appeared unhappy with Vic's musical career choice, and especially with his "Beatles" haircut. His look and musical lifestyle, though, made Vic a popular guy. "Everyone liked Vic in school," remembers Bucky Walker. "He was a lot of fun." Yet, in Neil's own way, he did support the group. When the Eddies were in need of a van to transport their equipment to gigs, Neil loaned Vic $1,500 to purchase the vehicle. Neil decided that he did not want his name on the title. At dances, the band charged a one-dollar entry fee. One morning, a cardboard beer box full of one-dollar bills, placed on the McMurrys' coffee table, testified to the band's success. More importantly, those bills went toward the loan repayment on the van.

Gayle was an outgoing and friendly student. Friend Linda Pouttu remembers Gayle helping her by including her in her social life, while shy Linda helped Gayle with her homework. Like her brothers, Gayle always had an after-school job. For a while she worked in The Knothole Boutique, a shop for young men at Bucky Walker's Woods for Men clothing store. "She was one of the best sales clerks I had," recalls Bucky. "She loved joking and laughing with the customers and they adored her. She also had a great work ethic." Gayle graduated from high school in 1967, finding her class work relatively easy.

Gayle also worked for Rissler and McMurry Company, spending her wages to buy half of a new Ford Bronco; Neil

Gayle in Casper the spring of 1970.

paid for the other half. To go with the new vehicle, Gayle got a St. Bernard she named Snoopy. This would be her first in a lifetime of many dogs, companions she held dear. Gayle's vehicle was much appreciated by her friends. It gave mobility to the teenagers and enabled them to go out and have innocent fun. Gayle always had lots of friends. She often brought them home and her older brothers thought that was great!

The youngest, Susan, was mostly home with just her mother during her final high school year. In addition to getting good grades she was active in student council, cheerleading, and in service clubs. She was crowned Natrona County High School's 1969 Homecoming Queen her senior year. During high school, Susan also worked at a dress shop and at the Bonanza Steak House, where she was required to wear a cowgirl outfit, which she did not particularly like.

Ellie was happy and content while raising her young family. But after most of her children left home and with Neil still away on jobs, Ellie filled some emptiness with alcohol. Her drinking would eventually have a significant impact on the family as the children moved on to college and their early careers. The love and support she had fostered in her children and husband would come back around, and be there for her, during these difficult years.

Neil and Ellie McMurry raised their children during the economic prosperity of the post-World War II years. This afforded Neil great work opportunities, which he seized. But economic times were not always good. Jobs and financial success varied widely throughout Neil's career. Looking back, the children could tell when the jobs and the economy were going well, or not.

Despite being away at work for long periods of time, Neil managed to be an active participant in his family's life. On long summer days in far-flung places in Wyoming, the young McMurry children would venture off on explorations, fish in the nearby streams, or collect arrowheads behind their dad's scraper making way for new highways. Yet, as soon as the school year began, they were back home in Casper with Ellie. It was a grounded, simple, loving, and predictable upbringing that would serve all the McMurry children well as they grew into productive and hardworking adults.

Vic's band, The Eddies, at the Exodus Club on Denver's Larimer Street in 1965. Left to right: Paul Huber, Vic McMurry, Swiften Shaw, Corey McDaniels, Don Teasdale.

CHAPTER 5
NEIL AND ELLIE'S CHILDREN BECOME ADULTS

At Neil and Ellie's encouragement, all of their children attended Casper Junior College, conveniently located close to their home at 1455 South Ash Street. The eldest, Carol started after high school graduation in 1962 and completed her junior college work in two years. Her original plans to proceed to an out-of-state college changed when she became engaged at Christmas to Bill Seebaum, whom she had met in Casper. Many college women, like Carol, returned from Christmas vacation wearing a ring. She followed him to the University of Wyoming in Laramie and pursued her degree there. Between her junior and senior years at UW, Carol and Bill were married.

In 1966, Carol completed her Bachelor of Arts degree in English and then moved to Ketchikan, Alaska, with her husband for his job. From there the couple moved to Kansas City, where Bill attended graduate school at the University of Missouri. Soon, children were on the way. Son Matthew was born April 4, 1969, and daughter Carla was born January 22, 1973. Carol's marriage to Bill ended in 1989. She worked in libraries for many years, starting as a shelver while in college, and eventually as a reference librarian at the public library while raising her children. In addition, Carol worked for the Wyoming State Engineer's Office library and for the

Facing page: Neil and Ellie's children at a Rissler and McMurry Company auction in 1994. Clockwise from top: Gayle, Carol, Susan, Mick, and Vic.

Right: Neil on the front porch of the home at 1455 South Ash Street in Casper.

Ellie and Neil encouraged all of their children to attend Casper College. This photo of the entrance shows the Administration Building in the background. COLLEGE RELATIONS COLLECTION, CASPER COLLEGE WESTERN HISTORY CENTER

University of Wyoming Family Practice Residency Program in Cheyenne. Carol married Pat Spieles in 1992.

Oldest son Mick followed an educational course similar to Carol's, entering Casper Junior College in the fall of 1964, then transferring after just three semesters to Arizona State University in Tempe. Mick stayed in Arizona only one semester because, as he admits, he had "too much fun and did too little work." He returned to Wyoming to complete his college degree at the University of Wyoming, where he earned a B.A. in business administration in 1968. "It turned out to be the absolute best curriculum for me," says Mick. "I thought that I would be an engineer and quickly found out that it was too difficult for a dummy like me. I just couldn't get interested enough [in engineering]." Lifetime friend Bucky Walker was Mick's roommate in Laramie one year. He remembers

going with Mick over to Carol's apartment on Sundays for her home-cooked dinners.

When Mick graduated from the University of Wyoming, the Vietnam War was at its peak. Classified 1-A and not married, he knew he would be drafted. Sure enough, in 1968, while working on a highway job for his father's construction company in Laramie, Mick was inducted. "We went to Fort Lewis in Tacoma, Washington," recalls Mick. "Then we went to Fort Lee in Richmond, Virginia, and my MOS [Military Occupation Status] was small weapons repair and supply clerk." The army offered him an officer position, due to his college degree, or the opportunity to train as a pilot. Both of these positions, however, required a six-year tour, and Mick was not interested.

Mick was sent to Vietnam, in the southern part of the country in Phu Loi and the Saigon (Ho Chi Minh City) area, where Mick claims "compared to other people I had a good duty." He was attached to an assault helicopter company that would fly troops and supplies out to the jungle, drop them off, and then return to base camp. "I spent fifteen months in Vietnam," explains Mick. "If you would do that as an inductee they would let you out when you arrived back [in the United States]. So I only had to spend a total of nineteen months in the military. It was a great adventure, but I wouldn't want to do it twice."[1]

Vic's Casper Junior College education took more turns and a semester longer than his two older siblings'. Despite the McMurry home being only a few blocks away from the college, Vic opted to pay for his own housing, much to Neil's consternation. To pay for his tuition and apartment, Vic worked for Jim Rissler, Vern's son, who had started his own business. This was during the uranium boom, with lots of mining activity. Vic assisted Jim with deliveries to his job sites. Vic also made time to play some music, though never again with his band, "The Eddies." He took several general college requirements while attending Casper, but his major interest shifted several times, resulting in an eclectic course of study.

Vic transferred to the University of Wyoming in 1967. The change in schools coincided with a change in Vic's interest away from the popular "hippie" music of the day to country western. The turning point for Vic may in part have been inspired by a Johnny Cash concert he attended in Casper. The cowboy mystique lured Vic into seeking, and ultimately obtaining, a B.S. degree in Ranch Management from the College of Agriculture, in January 1970.

Vic's extra college semester turned out to be fortuitous. By delaying his graduation for just a few months, Vic's draft status changed significantly. Starting on December 1, 1969, weeks prior to Vic's graduation, the United States Selective Service replaced its drafting system with a lottery, based on the birth month and day of men between the ages of eighteen and twenty-six. The original system had required all young men of draft age without legal exemptions and deferments to report to service. In the lottery, Vic's birthday, April 6, had been drawn 253rd of 366, giving him a low probability of being drafted.

Vic assumed he would be going to Vietnam like his brother. While waiting to be drafted, he went to Kemmerer and operated a Caterpillar scraper for Rissler and McMurry Company. At this time, Uncle Ken McMurry, a rancher himself, convinced Vic that agriculture jobs paid poorly and ranches were not interested in hiring someone without any experience – especially someone who might be heading off to war soon. While working in Kemmerer, Vic met and married a local, Jean McCloud.

Vic learned about the new draft lottery from the local fuel distributor, Art Piz, in Kemmerer. Piz, who was on the Lincoln

Mick in Phu Loi, South Vietnam, 1969. The woman is one of the "mama-sans" who worked on the Army base doing laundry and cleaning.

Second daughter Gayle, 1970.

Neil's assessment, and remembers one year she lived with the McMurrys while she and Gayle both attended Casper Junior College. "Gayle was just a sweet person," recalls Linda. "She loved life!"

Youngest child Susan also started junior college in Casper, and then in 1970 in her second year transferred to the University of Colorado in Boulder. Neil recalls, "Her mother and I went down there and we were almost afraid to stay in town overnight. I had never seen so many goofy people!" Susan agrees that the climate at the Colorado institution was much more radical than that of Wyoming. By now campuses across the country, including Colorado University at Boulder, were experiencing protest riots against America's involvement in the Vietnam War. In addition, drugs came to the University campus, and to make the situation even more stressful, tuition rose three times in the year Susan was there. "It didn't suit a girl from Wyoming well," says Susan. "In Wyoming we just drank beer and danced on the tables." Susan stayed in Boulder only a year and returned to Wyoming. She graduated from the University of Wyoming in 1974, receiving a degree in elementary education with an emphasis on remedial reading. She taught for twenty-four years as an education specialist charged with integrating reading into the curriculum in the Cheyenne school district. Susan married Doug Samuelson in 1984.

Mick married Susie Warburton, a native of Hanna, Wyoming, on December 23, 1973. Susie had graduated from the University of Wyoming with a degree in elementary education. Susie was working as a first grade teacher in Casper when she and Mick were set up on a blind date by her uncle, Dick Bennett, who was working for Neil as an estimator. Soon after their marriage, Mick and Susie adopted a daughter, Trudi, born September 1, 1973. A second daughter, Jillian, came to them as a foster child when she was three years old;

County Draft Board, advised Vic to not show up in Denver for his induction physical unless he was called. This information was invaluable, because the draft notice never came.

Middle daughter Gayle started at Casper Junior College in 1967, and later transferred to Sheridan Junior College. Neil explained her college career as follows; "Gayle wandered off to Sheridan and had a hell of a time. She got in a lot of wrecks and drank a lot of beer. She went for six or seven years and had a great time, but finally I said I wasn't going to fund it anymore!" Best friend Linda Pouttu concurs with

Mick and Susie adopted her when she was six. For twenty-six years Mick and Susie had numerous foster children stay with them, for anywhere from a few days to several years. Susan and Doug would adopt Samantha, a foster child of Mick and Susie's and the biological sister of Jillian.

In 1972 Gayle married Wayne Rosenthal, the son of a highway engineer in Kemmerer whose father had worked with Neil. "They got a divorce," explains Neil, "which was a shame because he was such a great guy." Later, living in Sheridan, Gayle met Allan Kinnison, who had two children, Jesse and Chelsea, from a previous marriage. The two were married, and Gayle helped raise his children, whom she loved dearly. While living in Sheridan, Gayle and Allan ran the Trails End Motel, which was owned by Allan's parents. In the early 1980s, they moved to Worland, where they owned and operated the Washakie Hotel. On Christmas Day 1984, Alan Otto Kinnison was born, named for his father Allan (though spelled differently) and Gayle's grandfather Otto.

When the oil boom "went bust" in the Worland area, the Washakie Hotel became an economic casualty. In 1987, the Kinnisons moved to Casper, where Allan worked for Neil at Rissler and McMurry Company, and later for McMurry Oil Company in the Jonah Field in Sublette County. Wanting to be with her husband, Gayle moved with their son Alan in 1997 to Pinedale, where she owned a business and became very involved in non-profit community organizations. Gayle passed away suddenly on December 17, 2006.

As previously discussed in Chapter 3, Neil had made it clear to his children that they could work for him until they were finished with school. Vic, having graduated from college, knew his employment with the Rissler and McMurry Company would soon end. Then came the day in March 1970 when Neil came barreling down the dirt highway where Vic was working near Kemmerer. He had good news. Mick was

home from Vietnam and in Casper. After a few days, Mick arranged to meet Vic in Farson, midway between Casper and Kemmerer. The two had dinner, and Mick suggested to his younger brother that they should start their own business.

Both brothers had thought about ranching, and both enjoyed working outside. Although Vic had majored in agriculture in college, he had already opted for a different career path. Mick admits that after his discharge from the military, he wanted to come back to Wyoming and "be my own boss. I wasn't certain what type of business, but when you live and want to work in Wyoming it has to be something in mineral development, construction, or ranching. I wasn't tough enough to be a rancher!"

Mick had managed to save three thousand dollars while serving in Vietnam, but since Vic had only recently finished college, he had no money saved. Mick offered to make Vic a $1,500 loan starting them off as equal partners in a new business. They both knew the highway construction business well, having spent their young working careers with their father's company. "We were long on experience," recalls Vic. "We did know a lot about the construction business, but we didn't have much capital." "We started McMurry Brothers Construction in April 1970," explains Mick. He had been home from Vietnam for only a month. "We borrowed our first note at the bank about April 14. We both got focused." Looking back, the brothers are amazed that they were able to start their construction business with only $3,000 of capital.

"I was pretty reluctant," admits Vic. "I have to say in the beginning Mick was the driver. I was always more cautious than he was." Neil did not put any money into his sons' venture. And, the sons never asked their father for money. They did ask him for advice, though, which he gave and they willingly accepted. The sons admit that their father's good reputation helped them with suppliers, who offered credit they might not have received otherwise as young contractors. This was the case with Gus Fleischli, owner of Fleischli Oil Company, a wholesale lubricants, diesel, and gasoline supplier in Cheyenne who had supplied Rissler and McMurry Company for years. "When Mick introduces me," admits Gus Fleischli, "he says my name and then says 'he is the reason I am here, because he carried my credit when I didn't have any money.'"

"I think they are good guys," says Gus Fleischli of Mick and Vic. "They started out on a shoestring and we helped them with that shoestring. We kept them supplied with products before they got their payments from the highway department and that was not any big problem with us at the time." Like many people in the highway and construction business, Gus was amused by Neil and his sons competing with each other. "It was kind of fun to watch them bid against their dad," says Gus. Father and sons were highly respected by all who worked with them. Yet, they were different companies, including their colors. Rissler and McMurry colors were red and yellow; McMurry Brothers Construction went with blue and white.

"The first jobs were what we called stripping pits," explains Vic. "We would take the top soil and overburden off the gravel pit, pile it up, then the prime contractor would come in and crush the aggregates to be used for paving. We would then return with the scraper to cover the pit. It was the type of job we could do twenty-four hours a day. We were getting paid seventeen cents a yard to do that. One of us would run the scraper for six hours, the other one would then run it for six hours, and then swap back. The only time we would ever shut the equipment off was when it had to have an oil change." The young contractors were taking advantage of the work offered by the second phase of a federal program in the 1970s that enhanced the interstate highway system. The timing of this federal work was very good for McMurry Brothers Construction, just as the first phase of the interstate highway system under President Dwight Eisenhower had been timed well for Rissler and McMurry Company. Mick and Vic also worked on reservoir projects for the Bureau of Land Management in Wyoming, as Neil had done early in his career.

Rissler and McMurry Company and another large Wyoming contractor, Peter Kewitt, hired McMurry Brothers Construction for subcontracting work on their large jobs. Mick and Vic also worked for McGarvin-Moberly Construction Company, a new Wyoming company like themselves. McMurry Brothers grew quickly. The company bought more equipment and hired additional people. Mick and Vic realized the more lucrative contracts were to be found with the Wyoming Highway Department. Their first highway project as a primary contractor came in 1971 with the construction of a runaway truck ramp in the Bighorn Mountains near Ten Sleep Canyon. They were responsible for excavation and grading on the project in preparation for gravel surfacing, which was done by a subcontractor.

"We really couldn't compete in the highway contract business because we weren't a 'full-service' construction outfit," Mick said in a 1982 interview with *Drive Train Magazine.* "Although we didn't have in-depth experience in the asphalt business, we knew that in order to competitively bid on full-scale highway contracts we had to increase our capabilities." This occurred in 1976, when McMurry Brothers Construction purchased an asphalt plant in Casper and the necessary rollers and pavers to perform full-scale paving operations.

The nation's energy boom, which started in the early 1970s, had a big impact on Wyoming and on McMurry Brothers Construction. Big oil companies such as Texaco were acquiring properties in Johnson County around Lake DeSmet because of the coal reserves in the area. The oil companies were also buying area ranches for water development. Local news media reported that Texaco had plans to build coal gasification plants in the Powder River Basin. Wanting to participate in this development, the McMurry brothers purchased eighteen acres of land in Buffalo with plans to build a shop there. "The big companies were out front and acquiring things," recalls Vic. "So there was a lot of work in Wyoming and a lot of people were coming here. The coal mines were being developed. That was a great time for a couple of young people like Mick and me to start a business. We grew really rapidly."

Vic and his wife Jean moved to Buffalo and purchased a home. Their daughter, Victoria Lee, named for her father, was born in Buffalo on September 14, 1974. About the same time, Texaco reversed course and chose not to develop in the Powder River Basin

Brothers Mick and Vic McMurry in front of their original McMurry Brothers Construction Company asset: a CAT 627 Scraper.

area. Vic knew he needed to return to Casper, where it was more logical to build a company shop. In 1976, Vic moved from Buffalo to Casper with his wife and now two-year-old daughter. Vic says, "I had heard my mother say over the years about construction: 'it's a good living but a tough life.' You travel a lot and you are away from home a lot. Mom and Dad figured out how to make it work, and my brother and

his wife figured out how to make it work." But Vic did not. In 1979, his marriage to Jean ended.

Reflecting back on the early 1970s, when the company was growing quickly, Vic says, "I remember my grandfather, Otto McMurry, talking to me a couple of different times, saying that he was worried about Mick and me because we seemed to be growing pretty quickly and borrowing a lot of

Neil with Ellie at their home in Casper in the 1970s.

money. He would go on to tell the story about Wyoming and the boom and bust cycles, having moved here himself in 1918. And, I remember saying to him, 'I know how it has been, but I really think it is different this time.'" But Grandfather Otto would prove right. The economic boom of the 1970s came to an end by the early 1980s. "Otto also used to say, 'it always comes back,' and he was right again," admits Vic.

To meet bank obligations and payroll, Mick and Vic consistently adhered to the same business practices that had brought their father success in the construction industry. They were always fair and honest in their dealings in every aspect of their work. Their Maintenance Superintendent, Dyce Brownlee, attributes their success in part to their careful attention to maintaining their equipment. This was another practice learned from their father. In fact, their toughest competitor was their father. "It's interesting competing against your own father for construction and paving contracts," Mick said in a 1982 interview. "Sometimes we win and other times they do; there is not the animosity present as when dealing with other companies."

The competition between the father and sons in business was not problematic. It was not unusual for employees to leave one company and go to work for the other. For example, Pat McMurry, Neil's nephew and Mick and Vic's cousin, was working for Neil when he chose to go to Europe for six weeks. When he returned to Casper, Neil had not held a job for him. So he went to work for Mick and Vic. "When I started [working for McMurry Brothers]," recalls Pat, "they were very small, and when I left they were huge."

Dyce Brownlee had worked for Neil for twelve years when, he admits, "I was thinking that I was working too many hours so I went to work for McMurry Brothers." Soon he was running the shop for McMurry Brothers Construction, work similar to what he had done for their father. "When I went to work for the brothers I said I don't want to be locked in the shop all the time," explains Dyce. After taking care of the shop during the week, Mick or Vic would have Dyce run a scraper or haul a load of oil or fuel on the weekends. He likely worked as many hours for Neil's sons as he had for Neil, but he did get out of the shop.

One of the McMurry brothers' earliest employees was their Uncle Dick McGregor, who started with the new company as its accountant. But Dick already had full-time work, and when McMurry Brothers Construction grew quickly, they needed someone else. They hired Bill Slattery, who was just out of college when he came to Casper looking for a job. Having nowhere to conduct an interview, Mick and Vic invited Bill to their job site, then took him out to lunch. Despite the lack of an office, Bill accepted the accounting position and ultimately stayed with McMurry Brothers Construction until they sold in 1988. Bill's wife, Linda, may have initially been concerned about Mick and Vic's ability to pay him, much like Ellie when Neil first hired on with Vern Rissler.

Economically, the 1980s were very different from the 1970s. The U.S. Congress passed a five-cent-per-gallon tax on gasoline to assist with the building of highways, and this was very helpful for highway contractors, creating plenty of projects. But at the same time the business climate was challenging. Interest rates for loans increased significantly, reaching as high as 20 percent. The price of gasoline and diesel also rose dramatically while prices tanked in all the mineral industries, including trona, oil, natural gas, coal, and uranium. Due to low mineral prices, extraction work dropped off and many contractors were vying for highway jobs. McMurry Brothers Construction was able to stay in business despite increased competition, higher interest rates, and higher gasoline prices, but Mick and Vic realized they would need to obtain additional contracts.

Mick's mother- and father-in-law often spent their winters in Phoenix, Arizona. In 1984, Mick and Susie visited them for Christmas; Mick took the opportunity to tour the area. "Mick was like Dad," explains Vic. "He never had hobbies. He didn't golf or fish, and when he didn't have work, he was lost. So he spent some time in Phoenix in a rental car

driving around looking at construction projects. He found out that in that county they had just passed a special half-cent sales tax dedicated to building highways and roads. He also noticed that they were laying asphalt in December. When he came back we talked about maybe looking into that market."

Life-long friend Jim Rissler had gotten out of his business, and was therefore available in 1985 to assist Mick and Vic as they developed the idea of taking on work in Arizona. "Jim offered to go down and be our front man," Vic recalls. Needing a place for Jim to live, Mick suggested his fifth-wheel trailer. The only place available to park the fifth wheel was Sun City, where one had to be at least forty-five years old to stay. Fortunately, Jim made the cut.

Jim was successful in obtaining work, and soon McMurry Brothers Construction equipment was on a Burlington Northern train heading to Arizona. Unfortunately, the equipment stayed on the train through Arizona and ended up in Long Beach, California. "That was the first of many [mishaps]," recalls Vic.

Vic would make several trips to Arizona to check on job sites and meet with Jim Rissler on whirlwind trips. By the late 1980s, it became necessary for Vic to move permanently to Arizona to be closer to this business expansion. Pulling up stakes was not a simple matter. Vic had married Robyn Loving in 1981 and their first son, Cody, had been born on December 27, 1983. Son Nick would arrive the same day four years later. Robyn, originally from Scottsbluff, Nebraska, had moved to Casper and grown fond of her new Wyoming home. She was not anxious to move to Arizona. Neil, too, was unenthused about Vic leaving Wyoming and moving to Arizona.

"As much as I thought I was prepared for this, I never had a stress level like when we tried to get into that market," admits Vic. "Arizona was used to having contractors move in from all over the country. In fact, they didn't like us very well. I got to know some of them and they would say, 'damn out-of-staters! You always take a few jobs and keep our prices low, and then you go broke, then you leave, and we are the ones that live here.'"

Despite the tremendous efforts to keep the company going, including the expansion into Arizona, McMurry Brothers Construction was experiencing real challenges. With the company split between two states, the operation was not as efficient as it had been. The Arizona construction market was also more competitive than Wyoming's, and both markets were tough. "I was in the office in Phoenix bidding a job on Sunday afternoon and Mick calls," remembers Vic. "He was out in Superior [Wyoming] trying to set up our asphalt plant. From a gas station, Mick called me and said, 'What are you doing?' then he asked, 'Are you having any fun?' I went on to list all of the troubles that I was having. Then I said, 'Are you having fun?' and he said, 'As a matter of fact, I'm not.'" That phone call made the brothers realize that what they were trying to do maybe "didn't make a lot of sense," says Vic.

The brothers agreed to a meeting in Denver, in August 1987, with their life-long friend and financial advisor Gerald (Jerry) Cornia, who knew the company's business well. Vic recalls Jerry told them that he had run some numbers. "I know that you guys like this business and you are a well-known company and well thought of," said Jerry, "and you have a lot of really good people who are counting on this job, but the numbers don't look very good. You're spending your equity." After the meeting the brothers decided that it would be a good business decision to dissolve their company.

After telling their wives, Mick and Vic knew they would have to tell their father. "We went to his office on a Sunday, where we knew he would be alone," recalls Vic. "He didn't look up. He was writing, and he said, 'Why aren't you kids working?' 'Well, Dad, we need to talk to you.'" They explained that they were dissolving their company.

"When we told him he just – the only way I can describe it is like we hit him below the belt," says Vic. "He dropped his pen and he looked at us with this surprised and disappointed look on his face. In a very soft voice he said something like, 'What are you going to do? You are too young to quit working. People can't quit working.'"

"That was the first time I realized that maybe he had some pride in what Mick and I had accomplished. I think a little bit after that Dad shared the rest of his plan with us for the first time. Ultimately, he really did think that someday Mick or I or both of us would come to work in his company, but he was wise enough to know that we had to go make our own mistakes, learn like he did in the school of hard knocks." However, Mick and Vic would move on to new business ventures, and would never join their father as partners in the construction business.

In 1988, the premier construction auctioneer at the time was Forke Brothers of Lincoln, Nebraska. Mick and Vic picked a date to sell their equipment which would enable them to finish the jobs already committed. "We had the auction on my birthday," remembers Vic, which was April 6. "I think our equipment went to several foreign countries and thirty or forty states. Quite a bit was bought by Rissler and McMurry Company." Neil was one of the first bidders at his sons' auction, and stayed to the very end.

One of the biggest difficulties in selling the business was letting go of the many valuable employees. "I thought that I would work for those guys for the rest of my life, but they sold out," admits Dyce Brownlee. Some went to work for the former competition – Rissler and McMurry Company.

The sale of McMurry Brothers Construction equipment took place on April 6, 1988. Neil arrived early and was the last buyer. He stands just to the right of center, wearing a red jacket.

Carol, Mick, Neil and Susan during a large equipment sale in about 1994.

Aside from their working lives and business ventures, personal events also impacted the families over time. The arrival of children brought great joy and new experiences. In addition, the loss of senior family members left a void that could only be filled with memories. Stella McGregor, Ellie's mother, passed away on August 6, 1965, from lung cancer, though she had never smoked. She was in considerable pain in the disease's final stage, which profoundly impacted Ellie and the grandchildren.

Huey McGregor succumbed to heart disease in 1972. Remembering Huey, Vic recalls that "he was a fiddle player. That was one of his joys. I had a period of time in my life where I tried to be a musician, in the 1960s. Grandpa Huey

was more supportive than anyone. He didn't understand that we were trying to play the Beatles and Rolling Stones music. He just had a real love of music. One of the things I wish I could redo – he would ask me if I had any interest in learning to play the fiddle and he would have loved to teach me. A couple of times I was with him and I had it in my hand and he showed me a few things and for whatever reason, I just never did it."

The longest living grandparent was Otto McMurry, who retired from Standard Oil of Indiana in 1959. He had lost his wife, Alma, just a year later and never remarried. Otto was a strong presence in the McMurry family until the spring of 1989, when he passed away at age eighty-eight. Neil and his brothers claimed that their father was stern, hard working, and "straight-laced," when he was a young adult. But later in life, Otto is remembered quite differently. Daughter-in-law Donna McMurry says he was "funny and so loving. Every day he would go to Frosty's Bar and visit with everyone. He was a delightful person. He accepted me and my family, and when we got together it was like I had been around forever." Otto's memorable answer to the question, "How are you today?" was "I'm coasting uphill." The family had his favorite response put on his tombstone.

As the McMurry children grew older and moved away, this proved a difficult transition for Ellie, who had devoted all of her life to raising them. She had also been surrounded by extended family while raising her children. When Neil was home, the many relatives often gathered on Friday evenings at the McMurry home to watch boxing matches on television. Ellie's two sisters, Mary Lou and Francis, were raising their families in Casper at the same time, and often joined in holiday events. The McMurry and McGregor families gathered for picnics on the Fourth of July and Labor Day, and for dinner at Thanksgiving and Christmas. Typical of the 1950s and

1960s across the country, social life often revolved around alcohol. McMurry and McGregor family gatherings included beer and Jack Daniels.

When the children were young, the drinking was not too apparent, but as the children grew and left home, it became more problematic for Ellie. After her work at the daycare, Ellie would come home to a nearly empty house. Neil continued to work long hours, and her children were leaving for college and beginning their own adult lives. The youngest, Susan, was in high school and old enough to recognize that Ellie's drinking had moved beyond just socializing with family, particularly when her mother fell and hurt her head. Neil, too, recognized that alcohol was creating health problems for Ellie. Concerned, he went to their family physician for advice.

At that time, the early 1970s, there were few treatment centers to assist people suffering from alcoholism. In Wyoming, the only available help was at the state hospital in Evanston. Not surprisingly, Ellie was not interested in going there. Neil, recognizing the increasing gravity of her situation and out of deep love for his wife, went with the family doctor to a judge and got a court order to force Ellie into treatment. In the fall of 1971, Neil took Ellie to Evanston, with Carol and her husband coming along for support. Neil calls that trip "the drive from hell." Neil has never had another alcoholic drink since taking Ellie to get help with her disease.

Ellie's recovery was slow. She stayed in the hospital for several months, with occasional visits from her family. Most memorable was Thanksgiving in 1971, when Neil and some of their children went to Evanston to have dinner with her at a restaurant. It was hard on everyone, as Ellie struggled to overcome both her addiction and her anger over being forced into treatment. When she was discharged from the hospital, Ellie's struggle with alcohol was not over. She came home for Christmas, but the temptation for alcohol was great and she began

Ellie, standing at center, with children attending the Presbyterian Church daycare in Casper. One of Ellie's greatest pleasures was volunteering with this program.

drinking again. Ellie then went to visit her brother Dean, a recovering alcoholic in Billings, Montana. He took Ellie with him to Alcoholics Anonymous meetings, which helped her.

Upon her return to Casper, Ellie continued her battle against alcoholism, and eventually won. She found the best help for herself with a support group led by The Reverend Irwin Brandjord, nick-named "Jug," a counselor for alcohol addiction at the Casper Hospital.[2] Jug recalls that after treatment, Ellie remained the kind, unpretentious, and strong person everyone loved.

Ellie later would discuss her struggles with alcoholism freely. She would tell her children to never be ashamed that

Ellie and Neil McMurry.

their mother got help, because she had been blessed with people who cared about her and supported her recovery. This openness was unusual for that time, suggesting great insight into her disease and great strength from her family's love.

One of Ellie's biggest concerns about going to the state hospital, and the stigma connected with it, was whether the daycare would allow her to return to volunteer service. When this concern was relayed by the family to the daycare director, she contacted Ellie and assured her of a position upon her return to Casper. Everyone around Ellie loved her. And when she returned, Ellie was able to continue her work with the children. "She really enjoyed reading and being with the children," recalls Jug.

After a decade of sobriety, though, Ellie lost a bigger struggle, this one to cancer. Like her mother Stella, Ellie developed lung cancer despite never having smoked in her life. Her father had smoked a pipe, and Neil had smoked cigarettes, although he had quit in 1961, well before Ellie's diagnosis. Neil has since become fiercely anti-smoking. Ellie had often worried that she would have a fate similar to her mother's, and unfortunately, she did. For Ellie it began as a tumor in her lung, resulting in a lobectomy, or surgical removal of part of the lung. The cancer then spread to her brain, and radiation treatment resulted in the loss of her hair. The cancer next moved to her larynx, and when it was removed, she was no longer able to speak.

It was a painfully challenging time for Neil and his entire family. In January 1981, Neil had bought out his lifetime business partner, Vern Rissler, taking on full responsibility for the business. As mentioned before, the economy took a turn for the worse at this time.

Interest rates soared to 20 percent and Neil had a big floating loan. This coincided with a market drop, resulting in less work available. A month later, Ellie was diagnosed with lung cancer.

Ellie lived almost two and a half years, but lost her battle to cancer on Mother's Day, 1983. She refused pain medicine in her final months, despite the suffering brought on by the disease. Ellie worried about becoming addicted to the medication, and therefore would not take it.

"I read once that one of the most traumatic events in your life for a long-time married couple is when one of them dies. Very true, it is true," says Neil. They were married for forty-one years. Susan remembers her parents' relationship with great admiration. "They had a great marriage. They were very supportive of each other." Before Ellie died, she and Neil talked about the future. Ellie made it clear that she did not want Neil to remain alone.

"It seems like every week something makes me think of my mother," adds Vic. He speaks for his siblings, as well. Extended family dearly misses Ellie, to this day. Her sister-in-law Betty says, "Ellie was the best, she was one in a million! I just loved her because I never had any sisters and she was the closest thing to a sister that I ever had."

Ellie was a strong influence in her children's lives, through her constant love and support. Her victory over her alcoholism only confirmed her strong personality. When the family lost her, a part of all of them was lost. Yet her influence, and Neil's, continues in all of their children's lives, as they become parents and grandparents, as well as successful business people in their own fields.

The McMurry family in 1984. Back row, standing: Gayle, Neil, Mick, and Vic. Seated: Carol, Otto, and Susan.

CHAPTER 6
RISSLER AND MCMURRY COMPANY AFTER 1980: A NEW ERA

In January 1981, Neil bought out his business partner, Vern Rissler, after a successful thiry-three-year partnership. Another sign that this was a new era for Neil came when he married Doris Roggow on January 7, 1984. Born in 1942 in Gregory, South Dakota, Doris was the third child, following two brothers. The family moved in 1952 to Nebraska where her parents farmed. Doris and her brothers attended country schools until the eighth grade, when they moved to Ainsworth, Nebraska, for high school. The Roggow children often spent summers in Wyoming while their father worked for various contractors, including Rissler and McMurry Company. They returned to Nebraska every fall to attend school.

Upon Doris's high school graduation in 1960, the family moved permanently to Wyoming, taking up residence in Sheridan. Doris met and married Joe Wenzel in Sheridan in 1960. Joe later worked for Rissler and McMurry Company and eventually became a superintendent. Doris and Joe had two children, daughter Kelly, born in 1961, and son Gary, born in 1964. The marriage ended in 1977.

When Neil and Doris married in 1984, they moved into his home on Ash Street in Casper. A few years later they moved around the corner into a home they purchased at 204 East

Facing page: An aerial view of the 1982 joint equipment auction of Rissler and McMurry Company and the Associated General Contractors of Wyoming. Approximately 40 percent of the equipment shown here would have been Neil's. He was selling the company's older equipment in order to begin updating his inventory.

Neil with Doris (seated), her son Gary and daughter Kelly.

Fifteenth Street and thereafter moved again, to 1030 Stafford Street. Doris's children were older by the time she married Neil, enabling her to travel with him for some of his business.

As the sole owner, Neil continued to operate the Rissler and McMurry Company under its well-established name. Many dedicated employees stayed with Neil, making the transition to sole ownership easier for him. Pat Bishop continued to administer the office as the company's accountant, and ultimately worked thirty-five years for Rissler and McMurry Company. Harry Rissler, Vern's brother, managed the shop as the equipment superintendent. He had started working for the company directly out of high school and would retire from Rissler and McMurry after fifty years' employment.

Neil maintained the company's excellent reputation, sometimes finishing jobs sooner than required. For example, on a 26.5-mile strip of I-25 between Casper and Kaycee, Wyoming, Neil's crews took advantage of good weather in the fall of 1981 to complete this section of highway. According to the March 13, 1982 *Wyoming State Tribune*, the Wyoming Highway Department noted that "crews of Rissler and McMurry Construction Co. of Casper worked overtime last fall to pave the highway between Casper and Kaycee, finishing that project in early December [1981] and considerably ahead of schedule."

Anticipating the partnership dissolution, Neil and Vern had not bought new equipment toward the end of the 1970s. When Neil took over in 1981, he needed to replace the older inventory with new. Neil held an equipment sale in conjunction with the Associated General Contractors of Wyoming. Buyers came to Casper from twenty-five states, Canada and Australia, paying a total of almost 4.5 million dollars for Neil's half of the merchandise. "[Rissler and McMurry] will continue operations with trucking, asphalt plants, rock

crushing plants and bridge construction," noted a newspaper article reporting on the sale.

All highway contractors saw a work reduction in the 1980s. Due to the recession, minimal funds from Wyoming's coffers went to highway projects. Furthermore, most of Wyoming's roads and interstate highways had been completed. Only a few earth-moving jobs – what Neil had done for the previous two decades – were still needed. Highway construction consisted mostly of widening and leveling roads to fulfill new regulations, but many of the highway jobs called only for resurfacing.

"Now most everything was a rebuild," says Neil. "You repave, or knock a few bridges down and rebuild them. The early standards were for steep slopes. Then the [federal government] came out with new regulations or designs, and you had to flatten the slopes," explains Neil. He also notes that by the 1980s, there were a lot of people in the industry, but little work. He was often the lowest bidder and continued to be one of the best builders. Don Diller, first Director of the Wyoming Department of Transportation, says, "I think a majority of the [Wyoming Highway Department] engineers around the state wanted Neil to get the work." They knew that the job would be done well and on time. In many cases, Neil was redoing his own early jobs. "We have done the first section out of Rock Springs three times," says Neil. He has completed other Wyoming highway sections three times now, as well.

Neil's honesty, integrity, and work ethic continued to enhance his reputation. In addition to working smart and hard himself, Neil had dependable, honest people working for him. "He hired and held good people who knew what they were doing," recalls Diller. "He demanded a lot of them. I don't think just anybody could work for Neil. He never hesitates to say what he thinks!"

Left to right: Harry Rissler, shop manager and equipment superintendent; Neil McMurry; and Pat Bishop, the accountant.

Casper's downtown along Center Street, looking south, in about 1983.

CASPER JOURNAL COLLECTION, CASPER COLLEGE WESTERN HISTORY CENTER

Gene Roccabruna, who succeeded Diller as the Director of the Wyoming Department of Transportation, claims Neil was thorough on every job. One time, while building a runway at Evanston airport, the equipment Neil used to calibrate the grade malfunctioned. The work, therefore, did not pass inspection. "Neil immediately redid it, and got it right," recalls Roccabruna.

A contractor could be compensated for having to re-do work when the state made an error, such as a flawed design. Some in the industry have suggested that a few contractors made frequent claims against the state in the interest of financial gain. These contractors would argue that faulty specs coming from state engineers had resulted in faulty work.

Once, however, Mr. Roccabruna urged Neil to file a claim to compensate Rissler and McMurry Company for extra work done due to the fault of the Wyoming Department of Transportation. "[The project] had significant design errors," admits Roccabruna. Neil responded, "I have never filed a claim in my life, and I'm not going to now." "You need to this time!" insisted Roccabruna. The highway department met, heard about Neil's case, and needed no time to make its decision. "They ruled Neil was entitled to compensation due to their mistakes," recalls Roccabruna. "Neil damn near fell off his chair!"

Critical to highway construction are materials such as limestone and gravel. Finding, and more importantly, being able to mine these materials, had been an ongoing challenge for Rissler and McMurry Company. For example, in 1976, the company applied for a mining permit for a gravel pit on land leased from the Rimrock Ranch, located a few miles southwest of Casper. Objecting to the permit were area landowners and representatives from the Wyoming Outdoor Council, Northern Great Plains, and Sierra Club, claiming lack of proper notification about the application. The original application was withdrawn and another submitted. Eventually Neil was able to mine the area, though the pit turned out to have an abundance of sand and little rock, limiting its usefulness. While trying to mine there, Neil heard complaints from an area resident about the noise made by back-up alarms on his equipment, which are required by law.

A year later, in 1977, nearby residents challenged Rissler and McMurry Company over a proposed gravel quarry near Jackson Canyon west of Casper. Of particular concern were the roosting spots for bald and golden eagles in the area. Other questions arose regarding possible damage to geologic formations and Indian artifacts, as well as disturbance of wildlife habitat. Neil opted to not pursue this pit, and never mined in this area.

This marked a new era in mining for Neil and others in the extractive industry. Starting in the 1970s, the public became more interested and involved in how mining work was being done by industry on public and private lands, leading to increased government oversight. Companies were required to comply with more regulations. The resulting tension between industry and the public would prove to be stressful for Neil.

In late 1990, the Natrona County Commissioners unanimously approved a request from Rissler and McMurry Company to rezone from light to heavy industrial a site near Highway 26 and the Old Yellowstone Highway west of Casper. Neil planned to use the area as a rock-crushing site. However, complaints were filed by nearby property owners that crushing rock would cause dust problems and devalue their property.[1]

Rock to be crushed at this site was to come from a proposed limestone quarry at Bessemer Bend, as well as other quarries. The Bessemer quarry was on state land and Neil held a permit for its use. Initially, Rissler and McMurry Company began mining the quarry under the ten-acre exemption law, which permitted the operator to mine within this relatively small area without the restrictions required for larger mines.

Despite working within the boundaries of state law, Neil's problems with the Bessemer Bend site began almost immediately. First, a local landowner refused a road easement across his property to the state land, forcing Rissler and McMurry Company to condemn the property to gain access to the permitted mining site. Soon after, other landowners

Neil with a rock from Bessemer Mountain, site of a controversial mining operation near Casper in the 1990s.

challenged the condemnation for this same haul road, but lost when the Wyoming Supreme Court ruled in favor of Rissler and McMurry Company.[2]

Wider public outcry arose when Rissler and McMurry Company sought to expand its excavation at Bessemer Mountain to 110 acres with small mine permits, disturbing forty acres at a time. Well beyond the ten-acre exemption, the company had to obtain an air quality permit from the Wyoming Department of Environmental Quality (DEQ). A local organization, Friends of Bessemer Mountain, was formed to fight against all mining there.[3] The group argued that mining should cease because the area included fossil deposits such as nothosaur fossils; nothosaurs were Triassic Period

Rissler and McMurry Company "hot plant" making asphalt pavement.

to the permit. Speakers were reminded that the DEQ had jurisdiction only over the air quality issues, yet the "emotional testimony frequently wandered afield from the specific subject, discussing traffic safety, water quality, economic, scenic, and quality of life concerns," reported the local newspaper.[5]

Representing the Rissler and McMurry Company was Donald J. Rissler, a Casper attorney who is also Vern's nephew and the son of Harry Rissler. "After reminding the hearing that Rissler and McMurry is a 'Wyoming company, created by Wyoming natives 43 years ago,' [Rissler] reviewed the economic benefits to be derived from the limestone quarry and the company's need to secure a reliable source of high quality limestone for the production of aggregate for building material," reported the *Casper Star-Tribune*. "'Limestone aggregate is a requirement on many federal, state and local projects,' he said, 'and it is anticipated within the industry that limestone aggregate will be a requirement on most future large-scale highway construction projects.'"[6] The lawyer went on to note that economic development in Casper would be hampered if inexpensive sources of building materials were not located within the area. Rissler also made assurances that the company would meet all DEQ air quality standards by keeping the dust down at the site, watering the mine area as well as parts of the haul road. The company was also willing to place asphalt material – for one-eighth of a mile – at the driveways of each residence along the haul road to reduce dust.

marine reptiles averaging ten feet in length. In addition, the area held historical value for its Oregon Trail, Pony Express, and old trapper routes.[4] The group was successful in getting Bessemer Mountain designated "rare and uncommon" by the state Environmental Quality Council. This designation, however, still allowed excavation that did not disturb the significant areas.

In October 1990, the Wyoming Department of Environmental Quality held a public meeting to hear comments about its issuance of a permit for the proposed Bessemer Mountain limestone quarry. Nearly 120 people attended, mostly residents of the Bessemer Mountain area, and most objected

Some of the public outcry against the permit maligned Neil McMurry personally and publicly. He responded by

Rissler and McMurry Company trucks load up with gravel at the Wyoming Department of Transportation quarry at Glenrock in 1990.

filing a lawsuit against six Natrona County residents for slander and libel. "Many of the defendants' statements cited as defamatory in McMurry's suit were made in public letters to state agencies, and in statements and letters to the *Star-Tribune*," reported the newspaper. But Judge William Taylor dismissed McMurry's suit, noting that recent U.S. Supreme Court rulings protected "fair comment" in matters of public concern when the comments "are not made solely for the purpose of causing harm."[7]

Neil's mining at Bessemer Mountain was within the law. After several delays and re-applications to allow for protection of "rare and uncommon" areas, the Wyoming Department of Environmental Quality ruled the mining application complete. But the protests, lawsuits, and counter lawsuits continued for years and cost the company a tremendous amount of money. The Rissler and McMurry Company ultimately made the sound business decision to withdraw its application for the permit, but not because of the permitting difficulties. Rather, upon further investigation of the quarry, the company determined that the limestone reserve was limited. There was not enough product to justify the cost of mining that area.

In an effort to recoup some of its expenses, Rissler and McMurry Company filed a forty-million-dollar "takings" suit against the state. The suit argued that the company had obtained a mining permit and was entitled to the resource. Thus the state, through the Environmental Quality Council, had effectively taken the company's property through delays

The longest bridge Neil ever built was near Douglas, over the Platte River, in 1985.

which issued the permit, and the Bureau of Reclamation, which was responsible for the water, supported Neil in this application. In addition, the Wyoming Department of Environmental Quality granted Rissler and McMurry Company an air quality permit. After attending to all the regulations, Neil discovered that the rock was not good and he abandoned the gravel pit.

By 1999, Neil McMurry had purchased a ranch in Alcova which had a dormant gravel pit. The Natrona County Commissioners approved Neil's application to mine the limestone, noting the mine site was in the middle of his own 700-acre parcel. Access to the parcel was on an old Highway 220 easement through the property. The nearest neighbor was almost three miles away from the proposed quarry, and this neighbor was Neil's brother, who did not object.

in the permitting process. The company lost in the state district court, and again on appeal to the Wyoming Supreme Court in 1992. Rissler and McMurry Company appealed to the United States Supreme Court, but the highest court refused to hear the case.[8]

Rissler and McMurry Company still needed limestone aggregate for construction, road base, and surfacing in the Casper area. In 1995, Neil submitted a plan of operations for a permit to mine limestone on a forty-acre tract north of Alcova on Highway 220. Area residents again raised objections, this time over the heavy truck traffic and the impact that blasting might have on water wells and irrigation canals. When all concerns were addressed, the Bureau of Land Management,

While the public used and benefited from the highways Rissler and McMurry Company built, citizen complaints made it difficult for Neil to obtain the limestone aggregate to actually build the roads. The local newspapers usually reported unfavorably on Neil's attempts to obtain permits for public works projects. Much of Neil's gravel and limestone for Casper area public projects was ultimately obtained from his own private sources.

In his continuous effort to expand and stay profitable, Neil McMurry went into the concrete business in 1983. Neil partnered with his cousin, Jim McMurry, and Jim's wife Alice, who owned McMurry Excavating in Evanston in the 1970s and early 1980s. When the energy boom went bust in

1983, Jim and Alice returned to Casper. Neil and his sons were bidding on the bridge by the Casper Events Center, a federally funded project. By now, federal regulations required companies fulfilling federal contracts to hire minorities. At this time in Wyoming, minority populations were sparse. To be in compliance with the new federal regulation, Neil and sons Mick and Vic formed Tierra Ready Mix with Jim and Alice McMurry. Alice is of Hispanic ancestry. "Tierra," Spanish for "earth," was used to represent Alice as part of the family business. The new company was the successful bidder for the job. Later, in 1988, Jim and Alice had an opportunity to move to Elko, Nevada, where more work was available than in Wyoming. This coincided with Mick and Vic selling McMurry Brothers Construction, so the Tierra Ready Mix Company was dissolved.

Jim and Alice McMurry's son, Ron, went to work for Neil starting April 1, 1986, at the age of thirty, and claims it was the biggest April Fool's joke ever played on Neil. "I mostly hauled equipment around the state to different jobs," recalls Ron. "Neil used to give me a hard time about the hours I got and how big my paycheck was, even though I was one of the lowest paid hourly employees he had. He said he was going to have to give me equipment at different times to pay me because my hourly wages were so high, according to him! I offered to take his airplane off his hands, but he declined. He kept giving me a check. I did that until 1990, when in Neil's terminology, I took a vacation and went to work for another company."

In July 1991, Neil asked Ron to return to Rissler and McMurry Company to oversee the welding shop, equipment

In 1997, Neil built a bridge across the Platte River at Fort Steele.

transportation, and oil hauling. Ron accepted the position, which included other responsibilities. "It had some added duties 'cause if you work for Neil there is no set job description. You do what is necessary to get the job done." In 1999, Ron would be promoted to Vice President of Rissler and McMurry Company.

Throughout his career, Neil has been involved in organizations important to his industry. He regularly attends meetings of the Wyoming Contractors Association, formerly the Associated General Contractors of Wyoming. Contractors privately fund this organization. Neil has given his time, serving briefly as a board member, and encourages his employees to serve as well. Neil has also been generous with advice and financing for the organization, greatly enhancing the group's ability to function and assist contractors across the state. Bob Gaukel, Past Executive Director of the Wyoming Contractors Association, speaks highly of Neil's ongoing support. "You could always depend on Neil," says Gaukel. "If you had a problem somewhere, Neil was willing to drop everything and go and help you. I am not sure if people realize even today what Neil has given to the state. He has given so much to so many."

Gaukel always enjoyed working with Neil, recognizing his gruff manner as a special personality trait to be taken in good humor. One time, though, Neil made Bob nervous. Neil had asked him to sit in on negotiations with a union representative who had a very rough reputation, including a murder conviction. "Neil lit into him," recalls Bob. "'You murdering son-of-a-bitch, have you had enough to drink this morning?' said Neil. That old guy just sat there and smiled while Neil ripped him apart – before we got into negotiations."

Gaukel's successor, Charlie Ware, also adapted to Neil's manner of speech. Early in his career as Executive Director of the Wyoming Contractors Association, Neil asked Charlie if he played golf. When he admitted that he did, Neil informed him that it was a waste of time. Neil also told Charlie that he himself would never agree to work for 250 bosses! Neil was referring to the Association's membership. Charlie also claims that Neil would call the office at 4:30 on Friday afternoons to make sure he was there. One time, driving back to Casper from a trip to Sublette County, Charlie was nodding off in the passengers seat after a long day. Neil said to him "do you need me to pull over so you can rest?" Charlie stayed awake.

Despite the barbs and teasing over the years, the two worked well together and accomplished a lot for the Association.

In 2001, the Wyoming Contractors Association honored Neil with its Charles M. Smith Civic Award for his fifty-eight years in construction and his fifty-six years as a general highway contractor in Wyoming. Three years later, in 2004, the American Road and Transportation Builders Association named Neil one of the top 100 transportation construction professionals of the past century. This award is given to recognize the contributions made by men and women who play a key role in the development of the nation's transportation network.

Neil McMurry's working life, from his return from World War II until the present, has consisted of the construction business. Neil's lifetime friend Bill Hurley claims that Neil has always loved the work, and could not have worked any harder at it. "In the summertime you wouldn't see Neil for two or three months," says Hurley. "He had upward of 300 employees to keep up with on his summer crews. He didn't delegate a lot to supervisors. He kept track of things himself." At one point, Hurley suggested that Neil hire superintendents to oversee things and report once a week. "So he hired a gal who took care of his mail," remarks Bill. "He is happiest when he has too much to do."

On Sundays, his one day off from construction work, Neil would sometimes try other business ventures, which he referred to as his "hobbies." One of these was drilling for oil and natural gas. This started early in his career and would ultimately bring him great fame and wealth. What financially supported his drilling, though, was his work in the construction business, particularly building roads, highways, interstates, and bridges across the state of Wyoming.

Neil, at right, stands with Don Young of Wells Fargo Bank at the Wyoming Department of Transportation Haebeck Quarry south of Glenrock, Wyoming, in 2002. Neil started a new company, McMurry Ready Mix, the same year, and would dissolve Rissler and McMurry Company in 2005 (see Chapter 8).

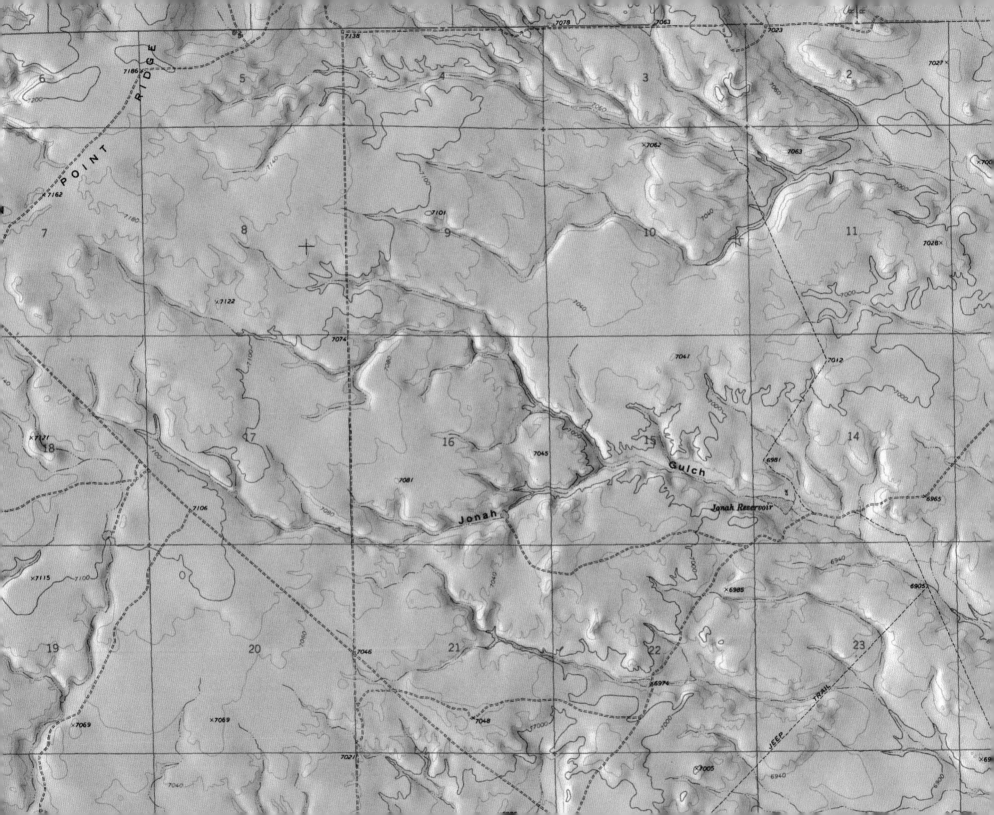

CHAPTER 7
A LITTLE COMPANY IN A BIG FIELD:
THE MCMURRY OIL COMPANY IN THE JONAH FIELD AND PINEDALE ANTICLINE

"We had a neighbor who was a wildcatter," recalls Neil. A wildcatter is a person who drills an oil or gas well in a region not known to be productive. The neighbor lived close to Neil and Ellie on Fifteenth Street in Casper. "He called me and said, 'I have a lease in Deaver and I have an old rig. If you put up the money, we can drill.' He had a gut feeling about a well, and in the oil business that is a sure thing." Neil thought, "Won't that be a nice surprise for my wife when I tell her I have an oil well for her!" He took $50,000 out of their savings account, and he was in the oil business.

It was May 1970 when Neil McMurry started in oil and gas drilling. "It was nothing very spectacular," recalls Neil when describing three wells he and his partner drilled in Deaver, Wyoming. But the results were good enough to keep him interested in participating in oil exploration and drilling, which his wife Ellie would later call his "hobby." When Neil told Ellie about it, though, she was not thrilled. His partner was known to "drink too much and had a reputation for being a woman chaser," explains Neil, and Ellie therefore did not care for him. "She hated the oil business because of him. She never warmed up to it and that is why I wish she had lived to see Jonah." Jonah is the name of the natural gas field

Neil's company was instrumental in developing, but that would be another twenty years away.

By the early 1980s, Neil was the sole owner of Rissler and McMurry Company and Ellie was battling cancer, leaving him little time to pursue "hobbies" like oil and gas. Recognizing his limitations, Neil devised a way to keep his oil and gas interests going. First, he reassigned one of his vacant corporations, a sole proprietorship, to oil and gas exploration. Then he changed the corporation name to McMurry Oil Company (MOC) and in 1982 hired John Martin to oversee the investments.

Neil, a Casper Airport Board member, had gotten to know John Martin when the board hired John to manage the airport. "I saw he was super smart," says Neil. When Neil hired John to manage the newly established McMurry Oil Company, he was unable to pay John much money. "I didn't have it," explains Neil. "So I gave John stock in the company with an additional override, if the company ever produced.[1] We were just hanging on, doing this work out of my 'petty cash fund,'" Neil states, spinning another "McMurryism."

Facing page: A detail from a topo map shows the features for which the Jonah Prospect was named: Jonah Gulch and Jonah Reservoir, about forty miles south of Pinedale, Wyoming. The prospect had been named in the 1980s when Presidio Oil of Denver acquired leases on several abandoned gas wells there. MAP BY BIGTOPO7 (WWW.IGAGE.COM). USGS WYOMING QUADS INCLUDE STUD HORSE BUTTE, BULL DRAW, SUGAR LOAF, SUGAR LOAF NE, TEAKETTLE BUTTE AND JUEL SPRING

This chapter will provide a basic overview of early 1990s conditions and practices on the Jonah Field and Pinedale Anticline, framed for the general reader. The topic is a complex and very technical one; the following information is not intended as a complete or detailed narrative. Moreover, it describes techniques used at a particular time and place, and is not meant to cover all gas field procedures, or those subsequent to McMurry Oil Company's involvement.

Left to right: John Martin, Neil, and Mick McMurry.

Martin recalls that his first working space with Neil was in the basement of the Rissler and McMurry Company office building. He had "an old wartime desk and an old typewriter that should be in the Smithsonian by now!" The 1980s were not a profitable time for the oil and gas industry. The price of oil and natural gas was so low that it was not economically viable to drill. "We were lucky that we had very little debt and were able to survive," recalls Martin. McMurry Oil Company drilled on a few small projects in Nebraska and Colorado, but little was extracted. Then an oil well in Potter, Nebraska, made them some money and kept them interested in the business. Neil also drilled north of Casper at

Sage Spring Creek with Bill Hurley, who would become a good friend.

By the late 1980s, Neil's son Mick became interested in what McMurry Oil Company was doing. Mick had closed the McMurry Brothers Construction business and was looking for another business venture. "Oil and gas was something I knew nothing about, but wanted to learn," says Mick. He partnered with Neil and John to drill a prospect at the Burke Ranch Field and some other small projects in the Casper area. "John was kind enough to explain the business to me," says Mick.

By the 1990s, federal emissions control was an issue for the public and federal government. Most of the nation's electrical plants were powered by coal, which emits high levels of ash, sulfur dioxide and mercury. Therefore, investors were looking for alternative energy sources, with most exploring oil. Recognizing the changing demand for energy, Neil, Mick, and John thought that natural gas would be a good investment. With great foresight, they identified natural gas as a "clean fuel," because it does not have dangerous emissions when burned.

"There were a lot of opportunities in [natural gas] and no one else believed in it," recalls Mick. John and Mick looked for natural gas prospects "that we could believe in and afford," says Mick. "We looked in Canada, Nebraska, and Kansas – fortunately, none of those came together." Then they found something right in Wyoming. It was called the Jonah Prospect.

"I happened to be visiting Presidio Oil in Denver one day [in 1991] and they were near bankruptcy," recalls John Martin. "They were going to sell a lot of their properties, so I asked if I could look at what they were going to sell." Presidio Oil owned three abandoned wells in a prospect named Jonah. Located in southern Sublette County in western Wyoming, the Jonah Prospect was about forty miles south of the small mountain town of Pinedale and approximately seventy miles north of Rock Springs. Because these wells had not tested as likely to produce gas, Presidio Oil decided to put them up for sale. John Martin convinced Presidio to let him review the files on these wells. Some years before, Martin had operated a well logging truck as a field engineer for Schlumberger Well Services. This work taught him how to read "logs" of electronic probes suspended from a thin wire cable down a well. This experience proved critical, because what Martin saw in Presidio's records convinced him that the abandoned wells in the Jonah Prospect were worth pursuing.

Making the prospective investment more attractive was the Kern River Pipeline, then under construction, with support from Wyoming Governor Mike Sullivan and the state legislature. Built by the Williams Companies, Inc. and Tenneco Gas Company in a 50/50 joint venture, the 926-mile pipeline would extend from Opal, Wyoming, about forty miles from the Jonah Field, to the San Joaquin Valley near Bakersfield, California. It was operational by February 1992 with a capacity of 700 million cubic feet of natural gas per day. The abandoned Jonah wells were located approximately ten miles from the Meridian Pipeline, which had been built years before to serve a few unproductive wells

McMurry Oil Company's logo was created by Mick McMurry and John Martin. The inner circle is the topographic symbol for a producing gas well. The outer ring is the topographic symbol for an abandoned and plugged well. The logo therefore represents the transformation of a nonproducing field into a commercial one. This image is now the logo of the Jonah Bank of Casper.

on the Pinedale Anticline, but were never hooked up. That pipeline connected to the Opal, Wyoming processing plant and would connect to the new Kern River Pipeline system.

In 1992, McMurry Oil Company purchased from Presidio Oil the leases for three natural gas drill holes that had not tested favorably, plus leases from the Bureau of Land Management on 25,000 acres in the Jonah area.

"It took a lot of guts to buy three old wells that had never produced and were ten miles from a pipeline," Neil admits. The venture was a gamble.

The history of the three wells begins in 1975 when Davis Oil Company, owned by Marvin Davis of Denver, drilled Wardell Federal #1, the first well. This well produced too little gas to be economical. Ten years later, in 1985, Canada's Home Petroleum acquired Davis Oil and drilled two more wells a mile north of the Davis well. Home's first new well, the Jonah Federal #1-4, tested at more than two million cubic feet of gas per day, but during the drilling process, or fracturing, the formation was damaged, impairing gas flow. Home Petroleum drilled its second well, the Jonah Federal #32-34, in 1987. That well fell victim to falling natural gas prices and was completed in only one formation. During the industry downturn of the late 1980s, Home Petroleum sold its leases to Presidio Oil.

Financing these abandoned boreholes and lease acreage was a challenge for McMurry Oil Company. Neil says he "and the bank" paid the purchase price of $258,000 when the second investor

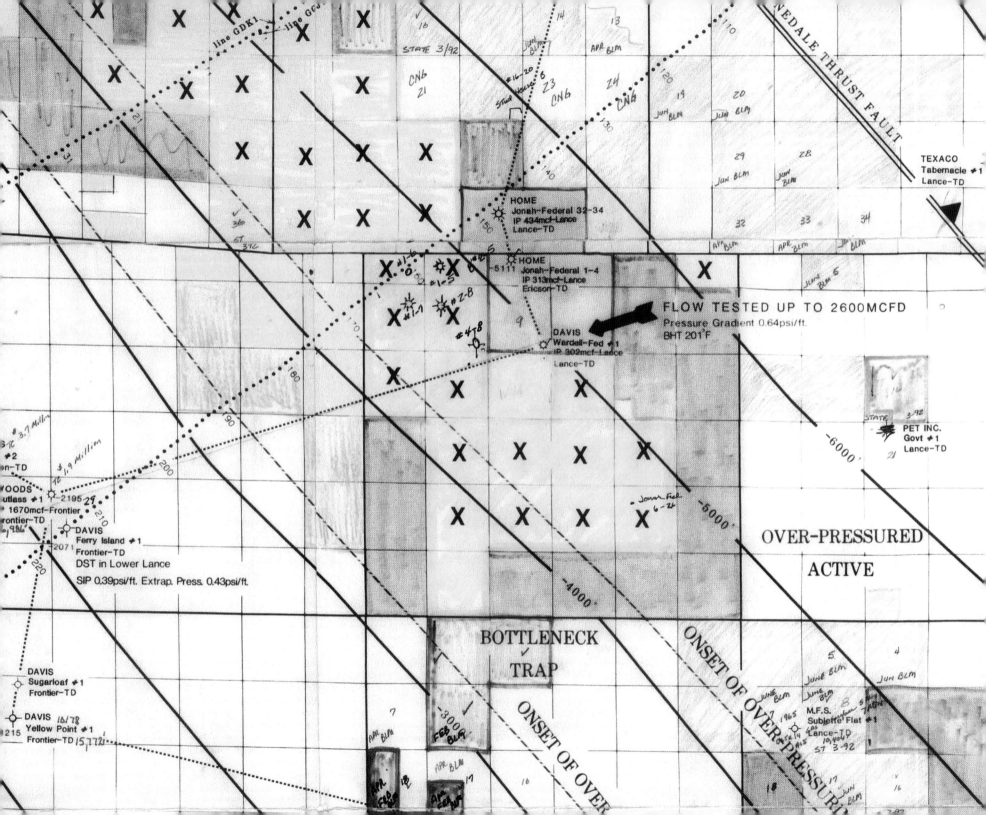

FLOW TESTED UP TO 2600MCFD
Pressure Gradient 0.64psi/ft.
BHT 201°F

NEDALE THRUST FAULT

TEXACO
Tabernacle #1
Lance-TD

HOME
Jonah-Federal 32-34
IP 434mcf-Lance
Lance-TD

HOME
Jonah-Federal 1-4
IP 313mcf-Lance
Ericson-TD

DAVIS
Wardell-Fed #1
IP 302mcf-Lance
Lance-TD

PET INC.
Govt #1
Lance-TD

OVER-PRESSURED

ACTIVE

WOODS
Cutlass #1
1670mcf-Frontier
Frontier-TD

DAVIS
Ferry Island #1
Frontier-TD
DST in Lower Lance
SIP 0.39psi/ft. Extrap. Press. 0.43psi/ft.

DAVIS
Sugarloaf #1
Frontier-TD

DAVIS
Yellow Point #1
Frontier-TD

BOTTLENECK
TRAP

M.F.S.
Sublette Flat #1
Lance-TD

ONSET OF OVER-PRESSURE

ONSET OF OVER

STATE 3/92

CNG

failed to come up with his half of the money, so McMurry Oil Company purchased the whole deal. "I couldn't do it all," admits Neil. Half of the prospect was then sold to Mick McMurry's new company, NERD Enterprises (National Energy Resource Development), and to Bill Weeks with Fort Collins Consolidated. They each took half, or 25 percent of the working interest, meaning they were also responsible for that percentage of expenses incurred during the entire project.

The new owners immediately set out to try their new venture, with John Martin managing the operations, drilling, stimulation (fracturing) design, and administrative responsibilities from Casper. Mick personally set up the production facilities on the three Sublette County wells. "Mick attended to the fieldwork, living in a shack, sleeping on a blow-up mattress, and eating 'beanie weanies'," recalls his father. Mick's responsibilities included location preparation, pipelining, and hooking up the production facilities. "It was a hands-on operation at first," recalls Mick, who operated the D8 bulldozer to build the road to the well, work for which he was well-skilled due to his years in the highway construction business. John and Mick enjoyed doing much of the work themselves, but it was also an economic necessity. They had little money to hire it out.

They were able to obtain help, though, from Big Piney native Casey Osborne and his father Jim, who worked together as independent contract pumpers. The Osbornes' regular route included the Luman Road, which went past the three wells McMurry Oil had recently purchased. When the elder Mr. Osborne noticed the new survey stakes proclaiming the

Facing page: This is a detail of the geological structure map used by McMurry Oil Company to plan its development of the Jonah Field. MOC obtained the map from Presidio Oil. The three earliest wells purchased by MOC are marked with an orange outline.

Top photo: In August, 1992, natural gas flows to a flare pit on the Jonah Federal #1-4 to bring pressure down before entering the sales line.
Bottom photo: McMurry Oil Company's first re-frac in the Jonah Field took place in November, 1992 at the Jonah Federal #32-34.

McMurry Oil Company's first wildcat frac took place at the Jonah Federal #1-5 on March 29, 1993, and was performed by Halliburton. A wildcat well is defined as a location that is outside known production areas.

After fracing, the condensate that came up the hole was burned off.

wells property of McMurry Oil Company, Casey gave the unheard-of company a call, drove to Casper to meet with them, and offered the Osbornes' services as contract pumpers. With some hired hands, Osborne helped Mick lay a four-inch surface pipeline to hook the wells up to Williams Field Services' Kern River Pipeline system. Casey Osborne later became MOC's field operations supervisor in charge of pipeline construction and gas gathering system operations.

Also joining Mick on the sweeping Jonah Field prairie was Joe Scott of Casper. When Scott was hired in 1983 he became Neil's second McMurry Oil Company employee after John Martin. Scott had worked on MOC wells north of Casper at Sage Creek and Burke Ranch. Scott then worked in the Jonah Field as the first "pumper," someone who attends to the gas wells. He was later the field production supervisor for MOC's Sublette County operations. "Mr. Scott exemplifies the work ethic Neil McMurry prizes in all of his employees," writes Jim Urbigkit in his newspaper series about the Jonah Field.[2] "Mr. McMurry claims the success of his companies is based on all of his employees' willingness to start early and work late. It's well known that if Mr. Scott started any earlier or worked any later he would have no need for a residence." Mr. Scott was typical of McMurry employees in the Jonah Field.

Significant geological challenges prevented successful extraction of natural gas from the Jonah Field prior to McMurry Oil Company's attempt. In Sublette County natural gas is found in the Lance formation, in sands laid down by meandering streams during the Cretaceous geological period, between 144 and 65 million years ago. This formation is "overbalanced," meaning naturally occurring higher pressure would force gas or fluid out of a well, even if the well-bore were full of water that would normally hold the formation pressure within it. The sand reservoir in the area is "tight," meaning it is not permeable, preventing gas from

Halliburton pumping the frac on the first wildcat well, Jonah Federal #1-5.

moving through the formation rock to the well-bore. In overbalanced or high-pressure tight sand wells such as the ones McMurry Oil Company was attempting to re-drill, gas would flow to the surface and produce a dramatic flare during drilling. But once the gas close to the well-bore had been released, the flow of gas would dwindle to little or no flow and the well would "die."[3]

Drilling fluids, usually water-based, are pumped down the drill pipe to wash out of the well the sand and shale chips cut from the formation rock by the drill bit. This drilling fluid also exerts enough pressure in the bottom of the well to prevent normally pressured formations from releasing the gas or oil into the formation, which otherwise would flow up the well-bore and in extreme cases become a "blowout."

Clean-up after completion at the Jonah Federal #1-5, April 1993. The structure at right is the separator/dehydrator, which removes water and condensate from the natural gas and stores them in different tanks.

Because the weight of the drilling fluid at the bottom of the hole exerts more pressure than the formation contains, some of the fluid seeps into the formation. In water-sensitive formations, such as those containing clays, the water can damage the flow characteristics of the formation, sealing gas or oil away from the well-bore.

To prevent damage from the drilling fluids, the wells are drilled "underbalanced." In other words, the pressure of the gas in the formation is greater than the weight of the drilling fluid, allowing the gas to flow freely to the surface where it is separated from the fluid and burned, or "flared." When the pumps that circulate the drilling fluid are stopped, such as when the drill pipe is pulled from the well in order to replace a worn drill bit, gas can accumulate within the well-bore. When the pumps are restarted and the accumulation of gas is circulated to the surface, large and spectacular flares can result. Flaring while drilling can turn into an uncontrolled blowout that might burn a rig to the ground. Preventing this requires extra attention on the part of the drilling rig crew members, called roughnecks, who operate and maintain the equipment under orders from the driller.

During the drilling process, the drilling fluid is chemically treated to prevent water loss into the formation. Heavy clay or bentonite mud is also added to create enough weight to hold the gas pressure back in the formation. This final step is critical to the success of the well in tight sands. Heavy steel pipe, or "production casing," lines the well-bore to the bottom of the well and is cemented in place by circulating the wet cement down the inside of the casing and back up the outside of the casing. When the cementing is completed, the pumps are stopped and the cement hardens in place. The condition of the drilling fluid, or "mud," must be correct at this point or the cement will not evenly displace the mud, leaving an incomplete cement job and creating later problems in well completion. After cementing, holes or perforations are made through the steel casing, the cement, and out into the formation to allow the gas to flow into the well.

To counter the lack of permeability in the tight sands, which trap the gas, operators fracture the formation in an attempt to produce channels for the gas to flow from the formation into the well-bore. This fracturing ("fracing") technology has dramatically improved since the first Jonah well was fraced in 1975. To fracture a formation, fluid and/ or compressed gas is forced at high pressure down the well and out into the formation fast enough that the combined pressure and volume cracks channels into the formation rock. These channels become conduits for gas to flow out of the formation and up the steel pipe set in the well. To keep the formation from closing back on the channels and resealing the frac, solid material is mixed in the "frac fluid" to prop the channels open. The most commonly used "propant" is sand, or "frac sand."

The first compressor station on the Jonah Field was rented from Halliburton and was installed at the Jonah Federal #32-34 in early 1994.

In tight sand fields such as Jonah, fracing is the final step in the development of a well. Fracing requires a small army of men and trucks to complete the half-day procedure. Pump trucks are connected to the well with temporary high-pressure lines. High pressure, high volume fluid is initially pumped down the well to "break down" the formation. The speed at which the formation will allow fluid to be pumped, measured in barrels per minute, becomes the rate at which the rest of the frac is pumped. At this point, the importance of complete cementing of the production casing in the well becomes critical. If the cement has not completely isolated the production zone, the frac fluid can escape between the casing and well-bore and flow uphole into shallower, softer formations. The benefits of the frac are then lost, and the well will produce as if it had never been fraced.

During the frac a variety of chemicals, compressed nitrogen, and frac sand are mixed as they are pumped. Maintaining

Left to right: James Shaw, John Martin, Joe Scott, Mick McMurry, Ralph Herbert, and Casey Osborne. The fracing had just been completed on the Jonah Federal #1-5, March 29, 1993.

computers. Nearly all of the workers on location wear headsets for communications. When the frac is completed, the well master valve is closed and fracing equipment is removed from the well location. At this point there may be over five thousand pounds of pressure per square inch at the well-head. Pipe is then hooked to the well to extract the frac fluid and any free sand from the well. It is then put into a skid tank where the waste is deposited in permitted disposal ponds. When all residual fluid and sand is out of the well, the well is connected to production equipment and gas then flows into the sales pipeline.

The three original Davis wells on the Jonah Prospect, which Mc-Murry Oil Company would later purchase, had all experienced modest success followed by decreased flow. Davis Oil's Wardell Federal #1 had initially tested at a flow rate of 303,000 cubic feet of gas per day. That modest flow quickly declined and the well was considered unprofitable. The two additional wells drilled by Home Petroleum in 1985 and 1987 used better frac technology producing somewhat better results, although production from both wells declined rapidly after initial flow tests. The frac fluid used on the first of those early wells, the Jonah Federal #1-4, had contained hydrochloric acid and water. Though the well

exact proportions of this mix is critical. If, for instance, too much sand is added to the mix at one time, the sand might plug the perforated holes in the casing and out into the formation, sealing the well. Called "screened off," it is expensive to clean this sand plug from the well. The result, in this case, is a wasted frac, and wasted time and money.

The entire frac procedure is monitored from a control van equipped with an incredible array of monitors and initially tested at more than two million cubic feet of gas per day, the combination of acid and water reacted badly with the calcite and clay content of the tight sand formation. This reaction caused damage to the flow characteristics of the formation, which caused a rapid decline in the daily flow of gas from the well.

McMurry Oil Company recognized that the only way to successfully draw the natural gas through the well-bores was to develop new drilling and fracturing technology which would allow the natural gas to flow freely through the formation. To this end, the company sought advice from the best consultants in the gas industry. It asked four top engineering groups to participate, then gave them all the information available and asked them to design a new fracture process for the Jonah wells. Two weeks later the four consultants were invited to Casper, put together in one room at the former McMurry Brothers shop, and asked to share their recommendations.

Martin explains how they conducted this meeting. "We started with one, asked them 'show us your plans and detail what you do and why.' We went through all four presentations and then I said, 'number one, what is wrong with the rest of them and why is yours better?' I did that with all of them. By the end of the day I knew how I was going to frac the well and who was going to do it." The job went to James Shaw.

Shaw also recalls the meeting in Casper. "They hired some consultants to quiz us about the Jonah Field. They wanted to figure out what the best approach would be. It was like a spelling bee where they would ask us questions from about seven in the morning until eleven at night for a few days until they decided that Doug Flack and I won the spelling bee." Flack, a petroleum engineer with the U.S. Department of Energy, had been in charge of drilling wells near Parachute, Colorado. Shaw had done the well completion

work on that project. Completion work entails supervising stimulation treatments or fracing, from designing completion procedures to choosing the perforations.

James Shaw was born and raised in Minnesota, graduated from the Colorado School of Mines in 1987, and became a petroleum engineer. Shaw first worked with Smith Energy Services for the U.S. Department of Energy in Parachute on natural gas well completions. The success of these wells was recorded in an oil and gas journal, which John Martin read. From the journal article, Martin learned that a young engineer, James Shaw, had been responsible for the well completion success. "For some reason, whenever James is on location, everything goes right," Martin was told.

At the time, Shaw was working for several different companies doing their well completion engineering on locations all over the Rocky Mountains. In 1992, Shaw was working with Smith Energy Services in Vernal, Utah, when McMurry Oil Company hired him as a consultant for re-fracing one of its three original wells, the Jonah Federal #32-34.

As noted earlier, Davis Oil had originally fraced the Wardell Federal #1 well with water, but the clay in the shale sandstone formation had swelled with the added water and constricted the frac channels. But after sitting for seventeen years, heat and pressure likely dried out the well, allowing natural gas to flow freely. A similar situation occurred with the Jonah Federal #1-4, originally drilled by Home Petroleum. McMurry Oil Company was able to hook both of these wells to the sale line without refracing.

It had been the hope of the McMurry Oil Company and its partners that the wells would produce one million cubic feet per day. To everyone's great surprise and pleasure, the three wells produced two million. McMurry Oil Company reported its first production of gas to the State of Wyoming Oil and Gas Commission in September 1992.

Joe Scott offers holiday greetings at a "Christmas tree," gas field slang for a wellhead, in 1995.

Neil explains that in determining where to drill next, they used son Mick's "roadology" geology. They went where the road had already been built. The new well would be a "wildcat," meaning a location outside a known production area. The site they chose was about a mile and a half west of the Jonah Federal #1-4, one of their original wells. Friends and family investors were brought in at this point. The first wildcat well, the Jonah Federal #1-5, was fraced on March 29, 1993. It came on-line producing four million cubic feet of gas per day, effectively tripling the field production. "Then we went south about a mile, and got a dry hole," recalls Neil. "If we had gone south to drill the first hole, it would have been all over."

The frac utilized nitrogen foam, which was rarely used because it put very little water on the formation. However, this approach was right for the Jonah Field with its sensitive clays. "We did it with a very light mud system," explains Martin, "and drilled underbalanced so we wouldn't damage the formation when we drilled through it. The trick was the completion, which Shaw figured out."

"It was just engineering," explains James Shaw. "You have to turn water into boogers [clumps] and then turn boogers back into water. If you leave them as boogers it is going to plug the well up. The Parachute job with the Department of Energy was the largest nitrogen foam frac that had ever been done in the Rocky Mountains. I like doing nitrogen foam fracs because it minimizes formation damage. The soap makes it easy to carry the water back out and it uses an inert gas that will not hurt the formation." Shaw adds that it was in his best interest to minimize formation damage, so the company would continue to hire him for additional fracing jobs.

Recognizing how important James Shaw was to its success, McMurry Oil Company asked him to work on future wells. "At that point in time the Western Company of North

America purchased Smith Energy Services," recalls Shaw, "and they didn't want to hire me and I didn't want to work for Western. So I started my own consulting company when I was twenty-nine." He named his company StimTech, Inc. He continued to work for McMurry Oil Company as well as for several other companies in Sublette County and throughout the Rocky Mountains.

The success of its first Jonah Field wells encouraged McMurry Oil Company to continue drilling in the area. Over the next two years Neil and Mick attended Bureau of Land Management gas lease sales, which were held monthly at this time. They slowly nominated leases, which was required before purchasing, and then often acquired them unchallenged for the two dollar minimum bid. They tried to buy the leases quickly and quietly, before other investors discovered their drilling success and drove up the lease prices.

Neil claims he paid for these early leases from his "petty cash fund." During the early years on the Jonah Field, Neil was not able to fully fund the natural gas work and had to use funds from his construction business or borrow from the bank. Because his funding was limited, some months he was able to pick up only a few leases. Fortunately for Neil, he had little competition at the sales. At this point, a friend admitted to him that those in the minerals industry were calling him a "crazy bridge-builder" because no natural gas could be extracted there. Within a few years, McMurry Oil Company had acquired 120,000 acres of gas leases in the Jonah Field and on the Pinedale Anticline, the natural gas field directly north of the Jonah Field and three times as big.

In 1994, the BLM office in Rock Springs issued its "McMurry Oil Company Jonah Prospect Field Natural Gas Development Environmental Assessment" which found "no significant impact" from continued drilling. This opened the way for the company to continue its exploration and drilling in

Eight-inch surface pipeline heading west towards Opal, 1994.

the Jonah Field. In an effort to raise needed money to develop the new leases on the Pinedale Anticline, McMurry Oil Company attempted to sell half of its interest in the field, but found no buyers. All the major gas drilling companies had left Wyoming by the 1980s, and were not interested in returning. They were convinced the Jonah Field and the Pinedale Anticline were never going to be commercially viable.

A break came when Snyder Oil Corporation, a pioneer in developing basin-centered gas accumulations in the Rocky Mountains, bought forty thousand net lease acres from McMurry Oil Company in 1994. Snyder drilled nine wells between 1994 and 1996, seven of which were completed as producers with average gas reserves estimated at three to six billion cubic feet per well. These wells helped define the southern and western limits of the Jonah Field. During that time, gross daily field production gradually climbed to about fifteen million cubic feet per day.

Shaw continued to do the completion work for McMurry Oil Company in the Jonah Field, though in the early years he also consulted for eleven different companies. "McMurry didn't want me to work for other oil companies anymore because I was only creating competition for them out in the field. They didn't want to make everyone successful. They approached me and wanted to buy my company, and so in about 1996, I sold them my company for a portion of their company."

In April 1996, McMurry Oil Company's final financing fell into place when MCN Corporation of Detroit, through its MCNIC Oil & Gas Company equity financing arm, purchased one-third of the McMurry group's interest. It funded a twenty-well drilling program that drove production from twelve million cubic feet per day to eighty million. Also, Vancouver-based Ultra Petroleum acquired a three-section farm-in, or carried interest, from CNG Producing Co. at Stud Horse Butte, just north of the established producing area, which would turn out to be right in the heart of the field.[4] The two years following these three deals saw some forty new wells drilled in the Jonah Field.

Snyder then formed a 50/50 alliance with Amoco Corporation to jointly develop its position. The partnership was a good fit because Snyder was experienced in reducing drilling and completion costs, while Amoco added value through its geoscience technology. "That infusion of interest jumped the Jonah Field into the lead in natural gas development in Wyoming," writes Jim Urbigkit in his history of the field.[5]

By 1996, Amoco had acquired two 3-D seismic surveys that were instrumental in delineating the field's key boundaries. The 2-D seismic lines used prior to 1996 had been difficult to interpret correctly. The 3-D surveys allowed Amoco and Snyder to drill wells within 500 feet of faults and to know exactly where they were going in the formation. The new data helped pinpoint the areas of highest production. "That's what made Jonah successful," observes Mick McMurry.

The 3-D survey revealed the huge potential for over-pressured production at 7,000 to 12,000 feet. Instead of drilling and completing the bottommost zone at 10,000 to 11,000 feet, the company expanded the completion zone from total depth to the top of the Lance Formation, that is, from 8,000 to 12,000 feet. By 1999, all the wells in the Jonah Field had been completed at these depths in the Lance and Upper Mesaverde formations.

"At first we thought this was a classic deep basin-centered play, which was basically stratigraphic," said John Martin. "Now we can see it's a combination of faulting – there is an important structural element as well as a stratigraphic component. In this deep basin environment, that came as a surprise."[6]

Jonah's estimated gas reserves kept climbing while costs declined. McMurry's first well cost the partners 1.4 million dollars, including one frac. A few years later a completed well with four fracs was 1.2 million dollars. In MOC's first twenty-well program, only one well was considered marginal. The best effort tested at ten million cubic feet per day.

Next, McMurry Oil Company moved north to the Pinedale Anticline, an area first drilled in 1939 with rotary tools by California Oil Company, which later became Chevron. Using only surface geology, these early oilmen had successfully determined where to drill, but upon finding natural gas rather than oil, had deemed their effort a failure. Later attempts to drill in the area failed to produce either adequate oil or natural gas.

In 1994, McMurry Oil Company acquired an interest in the Pinedale Anticline in partnership with Meridian Oil Company, which had a 75 percent working interest in the project.

Aerial view of the drilling rig at Stud Horse Butte #13-34 in 1996.

The remaining 25 percent interest initially belonged to Arco. Then, MOC learned that Arco's Pinedale Anticline interest would be auctioned in Houston, and sent a broker to the sale with orders to spend no more than $50,000. The broker was able to secure the working interest for $4,500, making McMurry Oil Company partners with Meridian, though Meridian was not aware that this transaction had taken place until after the purchase.

A new era began in 1994 on the Pinedale Anticline when McMurry Oil Company drilled its first well there, the New Fork Federal #11-8, which reached a total depth of 11,587 feet. The well produced some natural gas but it also had a lot of water. The price of natural gas was low at this time, making the well "non-commercial" or not economically viable. MOC opted to return to the Jonah Field, where it

Ground-level view of drilling at Stud Horse Butte #13-34.

Left: Mick McMurry with the "Christmas tree" at Jonah Federal #32-34 in 1994.
Above: Halliburton stimulation at Stud Horse Butte #15-29 in 1996. The platform at center holds production tubing that is placed down the well hole after fracing.

had plenty of work, and did not return to the Pinedale Anticline until late in 1995. In the meantime, Meridian sold its interest to Ultra Petroleum for over eleven million dollars.

With each new well McMurry Oil Company drilled and completed, new challenges arose, requiring ongoing refinements to its fracing techniques. "John was good about supporting me doing fracing differently than was standard to the industry," says Shaw. "I used weird chemistry, but it worked because it caused little formation damage. They always accommodated me in what I wanted to use for the

fracing." Shaw would make a point of talking with the drilling foreman and completion crews after his fracing work to learn as much as possible, and he used this information on subsequent jobs. McMurry Oil Company agreed to purchase the expensive pipes and chemicals Shaw wanted to use, unlike other companies in the field, who often used cheaper materials and saw less drilling and completion success. The McMurry Oil Company wells succeeded due to pioneering technology, and represent the first modern wells on the Pinedale Anticline.

Initially hampering drilling were limited pipelines, as well as a scarcity of compression facilities, which increase the pressure of gas in the pipelines and enable the gas to flow adequately. Mick's first four-inch line was replaced with an eight-inch surface pipeline. Then, in 1996, a twelve-inch line was constructed with a capacity of 100 million cubic feet per day. The following year, a twenty-three-mile, sixteen-inch pipeline was added to connect Williams Field Services, Questar, Western Gas Resources, and FMC pipelines to processing facilities. This line increased the daily transportation capacity to 175 million cubic feet per day.

On September 1, 1999, the Jonah Gas Gathering Company, a Wyoming partnership operated and partially owned by McMurry Oil Company, opened a new 50.5-mile, twenty-inch pipeline. This new pipeline would transport the majority of the gas from the Jonah Field to Opal, Wyoming, where it connected with the Williams Field Services gas process facility. From Opal, the gas was marketed into three different pipelines: Kern River, Northwest, and Colorado Interstate Gas. Completion of the Jonah Gas Gathering pipeline increased gathering capacity on the Jonah Field from 175 to 320 million cubic feet per day. Jonah Gas Gathering collected gas from wells operated by McMurry Oil Company, BP Amoco, Ultra Petroleum, and Western Gas. Plans were immediately implemented to boost capacity to 450 million cubic feet per day.

The increased pipeline capacity enabled drilling in the Jonah Field and the Pinedale Anticline

Drilling rig on Jonah Federal #2-4 in 1996.

Flowback at 2,000 pounds per square inch burning off methane and condensate at the Jonah Federal #2-4 in 1996. The process has since changed so that fluid and gas are captured and separated.

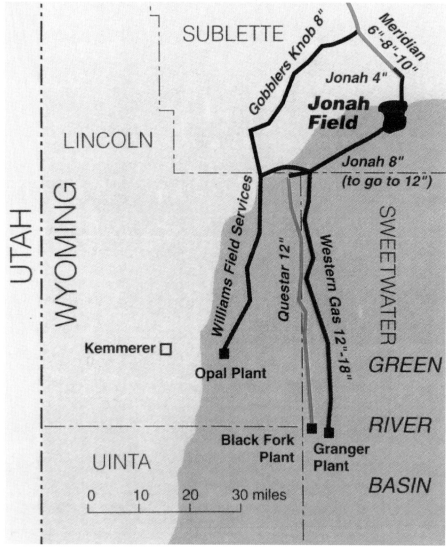

Map of Jonah Field pipelines in about 1996.

to grow at a remarkable pace. In December 1997, the Bureau of Land Management reported fifty-eight wells in place. By December 1999, there were more than one hundred and fifty wells in both fields and by July 2001, well count reached three hundred.

This rapid expansion was permitted by the Bureau of Land Management (BLM). Its April 1998 Record of Decision (ROD) for the "Jonah Field II Natural Gas Development Project Environmental Impact Statement" allowed full-field development. The operators believed at this time they would need 497 wells to fully extract natural gas from the Jonah Field, though the report noted that between 300 and 350 wells was "most probably" the number. One well was proposed at each drilling location, or "well pad." The maximum allowed drilling density was one well location per eighty acres or eight pads per square mile. The BLM estimated there would be 2.5 acres of direct surface disturbance to construct each pad, the pipelines, and other anticipated infrastructure. Full-field development of 497 wells would require ten to fifteen years, or about thirty wells per year. The total lifetime of the field would be forty to fifty years.

By late 1998, the estimated number of wells would be too low due to the introduction of infill drilling, in which drilling occurs between producing wells in a developed field to yield more gas at a faster rate. Infill drilling would nearly triple the number of well pads that had been considered adequate by operators and BLM in 1998, so that by December 2000, the well count had jumped from 497 to 1,347. The total field lifetime had dropped to twenty-five years, half of the original estimate.

In May 2000, the BLM issued the Record of Decision for the "Pinedale Anticline Environmental Impact Statement." This document estimated that each well pad alone would disturb 3.7 acres (five acres for multi-well pads), plus disturbances caused by access roads forty to fifty-two feet wide.

In the midst of the meteoric rise in drilling on the Jonah Field and Pinedale Anticline, McMurry Oil Company sold its interests. There were several reasons. To continue to expand in the fields, the company recognized it would have to attract additional major investors. Conflicts within McMurry Oil Company had also developed. Mick McMurry adds, "it had consumed us. We were getting tired."

By the time McMurry Oil Company began selling, BLM leases had become very valuable. Of the 120,000 acres put together by McMurry Oil Company, about half of these had originally been purchased at the minimum bid of two dollars. Now investment companies with deep pockets were bidding against the McMurrys at sales, eager to obtain lucrative leases, and driving up the prices.

In 1996, a twelve-and-three-quarter-inch buried pipeline was laid from the Jonah West headed north to the Falcon Compressor Station. This photo was taken at Bird Canyon.

One of McMurry Oil Company's early leases expired when it failed to drill there prior to the required five-year expiration date. This was due to a lack of time and money. The 142-acre parcel was in the center of the most commercial area in the Jonah Field. "By then we had drilled wells around it, so everyone knew that it was going to be a valuable 142 acres," notes Mick. Already planning to sell out of the field, McMurry Oil Company went to bid on this valuable BLM lease, realizing the auctioneer at this particular sale was unaware of its value. "It got to $32,500 an acre so we let Snyder Oil have it, but we were bidding it up," explains Mick. It would have taken McMurry Oil Company millions of borrowed dollars to develop the lease, and the company was not particularly interested in pursuing it. "We were kind of setting the price, so to speak," admits Mick. "So when [Alberta Energy Company] came to buy our other leases we said that the last bid for 142 acres was $32,500 per acre!"

In June 2000, Alberta Energy Company paid 741 million dollars for McMurry Oil Company and became the major interest holder in southwest Wyoming's Jonah Field with a 35 percent interest. This purchase included the Green River Pipeline Partnership and the 245-mile Jonah Gas Gathering System connecting Jonah to interstate pipelines at Opal.

An eight-inch diameter loop pipeline is buried along the Burma Road in 1996. Its purpose is to collect gas on the western boundary of the Jonah Field.

Smaller-diameter gas gathering lines are buried in 1997, to be connected to bigger lines farther along.

The *Wall Street Journal* ran a small article in its business section on May 3, 2000, which read in part, "Alberta Energy, Ltd., in a move that would make it one of North America's largest independent natural-gas producers, said it agreed to acquire closely held McMurry Oil Co., Casper, Wyoming, for about 1.1 billion Canadian dollars (US 741 million dollars). Alberta Energy, a fast-growing concern based in Calgary, Alberta, said the acquisition would give it an estimated 1.2 trillion cubic feet of natural-gas reserve in southwestern Wyoming, boosting the company's total reserves by 29 percent to 5.4 trillion cubic feet." In 2002, Alberta Energy would change its name to EnCana and become North America's top independent natural gas producer.

Other publications listed the sale at 616 million dollars for the gas leases alone. "Not a bad rate of return for drilling a well in an area that at the time was regarded by industry as geologically poor for reservoir development," wrote the *Rocky Mountain Oil Journal* on May 5, 2000. "In fact, McMurry had a hard time finding an equity partner in this play concept when the company was looking for drilling money. Among those who were shown the McMurry deal and turned it down included Chevron, Texaco, and Enron. Oh, what a difference fracturing technology makes."

"They offered us a lot of money," admits Neil. "We had enough money we were all not going to be on welfare." Because the company had given its partial owners and employees overrides, numerous people benefited from the sale. "They'll continue to get checks every month for as long as the field is still productive," explains Neil. "Overrides are just like robbing a bank and not getting caught," Joe Scott says. "The McMurrys didn't have to do that. I didn't expect the gift and it is a gift that has been giving ever since."

When McMurry Oil sold its interest in the Jonah Field, Mick McMurry and John Martin formed a new company, McMurry Energy. For a short time it continued to run and manage its undeveloped acreage along the Pinedale Anticline as well as in other basins within the Rockies.

Soon after, in November 2001, McMurry Energy sold its Pinedale Anticline holdings to Shell, formally known as the Royal Dutch/Shell Group's Energy and Production Company. When Shell bought McMurry Energy, it also purchased McMurry's NERD Energy, Inc., establishing Shell's presence in the Pinedale Anticline natural gas field. This purchase did not include James Shaw's original company, StimTech, Inc., or Mick McMurry's M & N Equipment Company, two service companies associated with McMurry Energy.[7]

The compressor station at Yellow Point, 1997. This compressor was quickly outgrown and a bigger one was built in a more strategic location.

On November 18, 2001, the *Casper Star-Tribune* printed an article titled "Giants benefit from small producers." It read, in part, "The recent purchase of Casper's McMurry Energy and NERD Energy by giant Shell marks the international company's first foray into Rocky Mountain natural gas in nearly two decades. In the broader picture, it also marks a clear trend indicating that major integrated companies are looking to the Rockies, and especially Wyoming, to be the leaders in future natural gas production in the lower 48 states, according to industry analysts. The big companies followed the 'little guys' into the Jonah/Pinedale Anticline."

Meanwhile, drilling in the Jonah Field and Pinedale Anticline continued, spurred by high natural gas prices. In March 2003, the BLM reported that operators had requested permission for an infill drilling program that would add up to 1,250 new wells to replace their earlier request for 850 new pads. Surface well spacing would decrease to sixteen acres, or forty pads per square mile. The BLM raised its estimate of surface disturbance for wells and associated infrastructure by over 40 percent from 2,927 acres to 4,225 acres.

Stud Horse Butte #1-35 in 1997. After five fracs, this well produced an estimated fifteen million cubic feet of natural gas per day.

in drilling in the Jonah Field and the Pinedale Anticline. As of 2010, drilling has never completely stopped and production of natural gas has continued, but at a slower pace. The field is expected to again expand drilling when the price of natural gas returns to a more profitable level.

The Jonah Field rediscovery and successful extraction of natural gas initiated by McMurry Oil Company is heralded as one of the most significant on-shore natural gas developments in the second half of the twentieth century. Jonah represents a turning point in natural gas production because the gas contained in the field is trapped deep underground in extremely tight sand formations. McMurry Oil Company's new technologies in the early 1990s, coupled with higher gas prices, allowed it and other companies to lucratively produce gas from a previously inaccessible source. This success led to McMurry Oil Company's expansion of the nearby Pinedale Anticline field a few years later.[8]

By May 2003, the BLM reported there were more than five hundred wells, which was over the number allowed by the existing Environmental Impact Statement. Additionally, these wells were installed in only five years rather than the ten to fifteen year estimate made in 1998. Satellite images graphically illustrate this explosive growth. The *Casper Star-Tribune* reported in August 2003 that a total of 3,100 wells might ultimately be drilled in the Jonah Field – 1,300 more than had been requested in the March 2003 infill proposal.

The national economic downturn in 2008 brought a drop in natural gas prices, resulting in a sudden reduction

Impacts brought on from drilling in the Jonah Field and Pinedale Anticline were not always welcomed in communities surrounding the area, notably in Boulder, Pinedale, Big Piney, Marbleton, La Barge, Rock Springs, and Green River. The influx of large numbers of people taking advantage of employment opportunities strained community housing, schools, and services such as law enforcement and healthcare. Concerns were raised about the impact the industry was having on wildlife, particularly sage grouse, pronghorn, and mule deer. Increased air and water pollution brought on by the growing industry also distressed local residents.

At the same time, considerable positive impacts from the successful drilling in the Jonah Field and Pinedale Anticline were immediate and far reaching. McMurry Oil Company employed fifty-six people by 1999, plus as many as two hundred contract employees. In 1999 alone, the company paid 13.2 million dollars in federal royalty, six million dollars in county ad valorem tax, six million dollars in state severance tax, $60,000 in state conservation tax, and 4.2 million dollars in total sales tax to Sublette County, for a total of nearly 29.5 million dollars. In 2010, Mick McMurry estimates private sector investment in the gas fields since 1990 has been between twelve and fifteen billion dollars, making it the largest economic project to date in the state of Wyoming.

The Bureau of Land Management and the Wyoming State Oil and Gas Conservation Commission requires every well site to have appropriate signage.

McMurry Oil Company's gathering system at Jonah – the Jonah Gas Gathering Company – provided interstate pipeline access for natural gas producers in the area, not just McMurry Oil. The company also invested in an expensive state-of-the-art 14,000 horsepower compression station that resulted in nitrogen oxide (NOx) levels only half of what the BLM had anticipated for the project.[9] This was because the gas burned cleaner, causing less haze in the area.

Bill Schilling, President of the Wyoming Business Alliance/Wyoming Heritage Foundation, reported in a 1999 *Casper Star-Tribune* editorial, "Celebrating Success at McMurry's Jonah Field," that gas production soared to 280 million cubic feet of natural gas per day by 1999, up from the McMurry's original two million in 1992. This accounted for 8 percent of Wyoming's total natural gas production at that time, with the accurate prediction of more to come.

Schilling concluded that, "What McMurry Oil Company and others are doing in natural gas exploration and production in Wyoming is important for Wyoming and the nation. Demand for natural gas is increasing in part because emissions from burning natural gas are a lot lower than burning oil or coal. Gas is being used for small- to large-scale electric generation, including electric power facilities. It's being used in the steel industry for blast furnace operations. And it is an abundant resource that America does not need to import. Some ten to twenty years from today, we perhaps will ask ourselves what were some of the turning points in Wyoming's economy as the millennium approached. One of those will be the discovery and the development of Wyoming's huge natural gas resources and the entrepreneur spirit of many to produce and get those resources to markets across the country."[10]

Important to the McMurry Oil Company was its employees' dedication throughout its operation. No job was too small. In writing about company employees, Urbigkit says, "When any of these men are asked about an underlying company philosophy, they all pause, then begin mumbling sound bytes as if no thought had ever been given to the subject. But if there was ever a case of actions speaking louder than words, MOC is it. This company, these people, personify the American dream. Years of hard work, dedication, and determined pursuit of a dream will lead to reward. Clearly, Wyoming's wealth is not the mineral resource, it is our human resource."[11]

Neil regrets being so busy with his construction business that he was unable to be more involved with the drilling work in the Jonah Field and Pinedale Anticline, leaving that to Mick and John. "It was a great experience," Neil adds. "I'm just sorry that I wasn't a little younger. I wished I had been able to pay more attention." He may not have been as hands-on as he would have liked, but Neil's belief, dedication, and financial backing were all critical to McMurry Oil Company's success.

"We started with nothing and played the big boys' game and won," says Joe Scott. "Without Neil McMurry, Jonah would have never happened. Neil and McMurry Oil is why it happened." It is noteworthy that Neil accomplished all of this with no formal education, having never attended college. Neil, with his partners Mick and John, believed in re-drilling when highly educated scientists said it would not be productive.

The story of McMurry Oil Company in the Jonah Field and Pinedale Anticline in the 1990s is one of triumph for American entrepreneurs. Starting with very little money and capital, these men persevered. Their achievement was the result of incredibly hard work and a willingness to take on very high personal and financial risk. Most importantly, they believed in themselves and their ability to accomplish what they set out to do – successfully drill for natural gas.

Facing page: McMurry Oil Company asked James Shaw to predict how much natural gas was in the Jonah Field, but when he provided the numbers, MOC made Shaw lower his estimate, anxious that investors would never believe it. His original predictions, however, were correct. This aerial view of the Jonah Field takes in the Wind River Mountains to the northwest in about 2000. COURTESY OF THE PINEDALE ROUNDUP

CHAPTER 8
NEIL MCMURRY'S 21ST-CENTURY BUSINESSES

When Neil McMurry sold his interests in the Jonah Field and Pinedale Anticline in 2000, he was seventy-seven years old and well beyond typical retirement age. Neil could easily have retired with the financial security that came with the sale. Since then he has continued to go to work every day, weekends included, using his profits to expand his business ventures and holdings.

In response to changing construction market demands, Neil started McMurry Ready Mix in 2002. Work for the Rissler and McMurry Company was transferred to McMurry Ready Mix, though the older company was not dissolved until 2005. Located on the west end of Casper at the old Rissler and McMurry site, McMurry Ready Mix supplies raw construction materials for concrete and concrete products. It makes ready mix and offers pouring, paving, and graveling services. The plant provides concrete to local contractors, as well as concrete for its own highway projects near the plant.

The McMurry Ready Mix plant is a busy place. In the yard is a gravel crusher and conveyor belts that move dirt, gravel, and sand. Trucks take on loads of fresh concrete made in the mixer plant. "Good concrete is fairly simple," explains Neil. "You constantly test the material that they are putting in and watch the product coming out of the quarry."

In recent years the operation has become more efficient by recycling old concrete, recrushing it for use as a base.

The headquarters for McMurry Ready Mix is in Casper, but the company operates quarries in Pinedale, Sheridan, Rawlins, Medicine Bow, Glendo, and other places. The asphalt mixing plant, cement plant, and crushers move to various job sites. Neil notes that to move tons of dirt, gravel, and concrete, federal regulations require "a ton of records! You have to keep information on every truck and every truck driver. You have to hire extra help just for the paperwork!"

While Neil has remained the majority stockholder in McMurry Ready Mix Company, for years he has been bringing dedicated employees, some of whom are relatives, on as business owners. Ron McMurry, son of Alice and Jim, took advantage of the opportunity to become a minority stockholder starting in 1999 and was promoted to Vice President, a position he currently holds. Neil's nephew Pat McMurry, also a dedicated employee, became a company owner, too. "We were given an opportunity by Neil to buy into the company – that would never have happened without him," notes Pat.

Non-family employees also became partial owners in McMurry Ready Mix Company. Curt Hovet has worked for Neil for over two decades, becoming the General Superintendent

Facing page: McMurry Ready Mix was established in 2002. The plant is on the west side of Casper, occupying the former site of Rissler and McMurry Company. The large structure at center is the clarifier, which cleans water for reuse after washing sand to make concrete. ANN NOBLE PHOTO

McMurry Ready Mix batch plant and cement silos in Casper. This facility mixes rock, sand, water, cement and additives to make concrete. ANN NOBLE PHOTO

highway construction and site work." Dean Lewin, in charge of concrete at the ready mix plant, has been with the company since 2002. Lewin joins the company's owners and employees devoted to keeping its competitive edge and to maintaining its claim as "the supplier of the finest raw materials for concrete and concrete products at cost-effective prices."

Although the McMurry Ready Mix office, shop, and yard are located on the west side of Casper, Neil has been responsible for much of the town's development on its east side. As early as 1977, Neil, his partner Vern Rissler, Neil's sons, and Bob and Bill Barnard were interested in developing property at the Hat Six interchange on I-25, but the poor economy of the 1980s stalled it. "So I sat on these lots for thirty years!" explains Neil.

Formidable development on the east end of Casper began when Neil, through his new company, Eastgate Ranch LLC, purchased the 2,700-acre Bentley Ranch from James and Pamela Bentley in September 2000. The property is located along Interstate Highway 25 west of Hat Six Road and was described at the time of purchase by the local newspaper as "in the path of the booming retail development along Second Street."[1]

Neil and son Mick recognized the logical extension of town east along Second Street. Mick purchased property from Betty Lou and Bill Luker between the Bentley Ranch and what was at that time the east end of Casper. In addition to being near the Eastridge Shopping Mall, the Luker and Bentley properties were adjacent to I-25 where major businesses would want to be located.

and partial owner in McMurry Ready Mix and other companies owned by Neil. Juan Freire, who came to Wyoming from Spain when he married a local college Spanish teacher, works for Neil as an accountant and is also an owner in several companies with him. "He's an absolute whiz," claims Neil, "but hard to understand!" Neil is referring to Juan's strong Spanish accent. "He hardly ever makes a mistake, and he can make excellent projections."

On its website, McMurry Ready Mix describes itself as "one of the largest aggregate producers in the State of Wyoming. We have a large fleet of various construction equipment and trucks able to handle almost any size project. Our supervisory staff has over fifty years of experience in heavy

Many Casper citizens and city officials, arguing that Casper had enough business districts, did not support Neil's suggested business extension of Second Street from the east end of town. In 2003, Neil pursued his development by first giving the state the right of way for the street, and then building the road with Bill Luker. Neil bid very low to build this street, paying for most of it himself. He wanted to ensure that it would get done quickly. "I didn't make any money on it, but I knew if someone else got the job they might stall it for a year and I wanted it done now," explains Neil. "So we got right on it. We punched it through and paved it, then started selling lots."

Neil brought a variety of enterprises into the 500-acre area, which would soon be known as McMurry Business Park. The first businesses were car dealerships. Coliseum Motor Company, a dealer for Chrysler, Jeep, and Dodge vehicles, opened adjacent to Big Wyoming, a dealer for Cadillac, Buick, Pontiac, and GMC. As part of the Coliseum Motor Company deal, Neil accepted the old Coliseum Motor Company building in downtown Casper in trade for part of the purchase price.

On the new east Second Street, several more businesses soon moved in. Menards, a 230,000-square-foot home improvement store, arrived about the same time as FireRock Steak House and two hotels, a Holiday Inn and a MainStay Suites. Medical facilities in the development include the new Mountain View Regional Hospital, Therapy Solutions, and Rocky Mountain Oncology.

The McMurry Business Park also comprises business centers and office complexes. Seven different buildings make up the Foothills Professional Offices, including law offices,

Neil and Mick McMurry, center, are flanked by Bill and Betty Lou Luker at the October 2003 opening of the east Second Street extension in Casper. Today the empty spaces on either side of the road have seen significant development.

The entrances to the McMurry Business Park on east Second Street are marked by these signs. ANN NOBLE PHOTO

Neil with his daughters (left to right): Gayle, Susan and Carol, in a McMurry Ready Mix shop.

At the Hat Six Road on I-25 there used to be a small truck stop. It had been built in the 1980s and was not doing well when Neil moved into the area. Neil and Doris purchased it in February 2001, then set out to expand and upgrade it. Their plans included adding a new restaurant and a liquor store adjacent to a convenience store. Neil and Doris also wanted to expand pumps and parking for truckers.

To do the renovation, Neil hired Rich Fairservis, a Casper contractor. "Being as frugal as he is," recalls Rich, "we decided to build over the existing facility. He just couldn't bring himself to scrap the old building and build next door." Rich also recalls that Neil visited the job site every day, in keeping with his lifelong practice. Since its re-opening, Neil and Doris have been regular patrons, supporting and encouraging the employees.

Fairservis' work for Neil at the truck stop was so successful that the

medical practices, and a mortgage company. The Enterprise Center is another multi-tenant office complex. The Park Ridge Professional Center houses the New York Life Insurance Company's regional office. In addition, the Granite Peak Business Center is home to W. N. McMurry Construction Company and Granite Peak Development, two companies of which Neil is a principal. Current plans for the McMurry Business Park include more medical facilities, hotels, shops, and restaurants.[2]

two went into partnership in 2002 on a residential project in Bar Nunn which they called the Vista Hills Subdivision. For this 50/50 venture Neil and Rich formed the company Bar Nunn Development, a precursor to Granite Peak Development LLC. On 600 acres Neil had purchased in the mid-1990s, the company built three hundred single-family residences. The usual obstacles presented themselves before construction could begin, such as completing the engineering and getting necessary approvals from the Bar Nunn

McMurry Ready Mix constructing the Professional Office Center on east Second Street in 2007.

Granite Peak Development LLC, Magnum Construction Company, and W. N. McMurry Construction Company are some of the new business ventures that Neil has created since 2000. These businesses have been housed since 2008 in the Granite Peak Business Center, pictured at right. BURT WIDMER PHOTO

Planning and Zoning Department. Bar Nunn had its own sewer system while Wardwell, the adjacent small community, owned the water for the area. The two municipalities rarely worked well together, making this stage difficult for Fairservis. According to Rich, the meetings between the two cities would go better when Neil was present, and credits him with ultimately obtaining the needed permits.

Neil and Rich built Vista Hills at a time when Casper had a great need for affordable housing for middle income earners. Neil and Rich sold three hundred homes in four years. The first home was built for Neil's sister-in-law, Betty McMurry, who had married Neil's youngest brother, Donald,

and was by now a widow. Given the project's success, community leaders asked Neil and Rich to build additional subdivisions. Constructing more homes in Bar Nunn, however, was hampered by a shortage of water and water pressure to the area.

Fortunately, other areas became available for much-needed housing. Neil and Rich built two subdivisions with a total of 112 single-family residential lots near the McMurry Business Park. These subdivisions, Park Ridge Village and Park Ridge Estates, were built by their new company, Granite Peak Development LLC, with minority owners Dan Guerttman, Ron McMurry, Pat McMurry, Juan Freire and Bob West. The company also constructed Eagle Estates, a 243-home project in Evansville. Some units in each of the developments were sold to employees working for Neil.

Within a few years, Granite Peak Development became one of Wyoming's largest developers of residential and commercial real estate. Named after a very hard rock and symbolizing Neil's lifetime of work with rock, the company owns, develops, constructs, leases, manages, and sells commercial, retail, industrial, and residential properties throughout Casper and Natrona County.

In 2002, yet another new company was formed: W. N. McMurry Construction. It performs general contracting, construction management, and design/build work. Rich and Neil are the principal owners, with minority owners Rick Nelson, Ron McMurry, and Pat McMurry. It completed much of the commercial construction for Granite Peak Development. The company's website states, "Our company has the ability to coordinate the planning, design, marketing, and financing of a broad range of commercial projects." Its mission statement reads in part, "W. N. McMurry Construction Company is committed to community involvement and building a better Wyoming by providing jobs and needed services." The company has built Granite Peak Business Center, FireRock Steak House, Honda of Casper, Halliburton Sperry Building, St. Anthony Tri-Parish School, Park Ridge Medical, Rocky Mountain Oncology, and the Park Ridge Professional Center, among other facilities.

Neil and Rich are also the principal owners of Magnum Construction LLC which specializes in concrete surfacing and foundations. The original owner was retiring, so Neil and Rich purchased the company, which has done well. They have refined concrete to the point that they offer a highly technical product particularly well suited for specialty foundations and footings.

New trucks in the yard at McMurry Ready Mix in 2008.

McMurry Ready Mix yard. ANN NOBLE PHOTO

This 2010 aerial view shows the Casper Logistics Hub, or C-Tran, adjacent to the Natrona County International Airport. Here, parts of wind turbines are readied for transport. BURT WIDMER PHOTO

to the County for the rail spur; and the County owned the railroad siding. The project was paid for in part with a 1.5-million-dollar Business Ready Community Grant from the State, and the balance of the 2.4-million-dollar project was paid for by Bishop Industrial Rail Park.

The rail spur includes two turnouts and is long enough to accommodate a unit train, which is usually 110 cars. The transloading facility, located along the mainline of the Burlington Northern Santa Fe west of town, is expected to handle over 12,000 rail cars annually. Transloading is the process of transferring either railroad freight containers to semi-trucks, or loading truck freight onto rail cars. Future plans include an industrial park to accompany this rail facility, with water, sewer, and upgraded roads, electricity, natural gas, and telecommunications.

The rail spur and transloading facility in the Casper area will serve all of central Wyoming. It will be the largest transloading facility between Denver, Colorado and Laurel, Montana. No other rail yard in Wyoming is able to meet current and anticipated demand for the receipt or shipment of bulk freight. "The need for an Industrial Zoned Trans-Load facility in Central Wyoming is well documented and becoming readily apparent," the Wyoming Business Council, a partner in the project, wrote in early 2008. "With increases in industrial and commercial

In 2006, Granite Peak Development purchased the Bishop Industrial Rail Park, 700 acres of land adjacent to the Natrona County International Airport, and re-named it Casper Transloading or "C-Tran." It is also known as the Casper Logistics Hub.[3] On this site the company completed an 8,500-foot-long rail spur off the main line of the Burlington Northern Santa Fe Railroad in August 2008. This was a joint project between Natrona County and Bishop Industrial Rail Park LLC. Bishop donated the right-of-way construction, petroleum and raw commodity industries, and the economics associated with rail transport, the demand is continually growing."[4]

Neil wants to connect his rail venture in Casper to one in Cheyenne, the state capitol. Ground was broken there in 2009 for a transloading facility and new industrial and commercial hub. Granite Peak is developing this facility south of I-80 and adjacent to I-25. The site is bracketed by Union Pacific tracks along its western border and Burlington Northern Santa Fe (BNSF) tracks to the east. Located on part of the Swan Ranch, owned by Neil and his daughters, it is now called the Cheyenne Logistics Hub at Swan Ranch. This 900-acre project will have a 10,000-foot rail spur connecting transloading activities inside the park to the Burlington Northern rail system, with hopes that the Union Pacific Railroad will become active at the hub as well. Development plans are also in the works for the southwest side of Cheyenne. Granite Peak wants to build a 1,500-acre business park there much like the one it built in Casper, with residential, commercial, and industrial components.

The two transloading facilities Neil has helped develop are expected to attract different types of businesses and opportunities to the Wyoming marketplace. The Casper hub is anticipated to conduct more energy-related activities, such as oil, gas, and wind, while Cheyenne is expected to attract manufacturing, warehousing, and commercial businesses. Both areas are projected to continue to grow in the near future, stimulating the state's economy.[5]

Yet another business venture Neil has taken on in recent years is the purchase of ranches, sometimes for agriculture and sometimes not. Starting back in the mid-1990s, Neil purchased a ranch in Alcova, primarily for the quarry on the property (see Chapter 6). He was in constant need of limestone and other aggregates for his highway construction and

McMurry Ready Mix helped Union Cellular install cell phone towers on Pumpkin Buttes in 2007. CATs were used to pull the cement trucks up to the tower sites.

other building projects. This quarry enabled him to obtain the much-needed raw materials without the difficult process of obtaining it on public lands. Neil also admits purchasing the Alcova Ranch as a real estate investment. "You can put one hundred dollars into a CD or bond and get one hundred dollars back," explains Neil, "but that one hundred dollars won't buy as much as it did when you put the money in."

With his three daughters and their husbands, Neil purchased the historic Warren Livestock Company in August of 2000. Founded in 1897 by Senator Francis Warren, the state's first governor and one of its first two United States senators, the ranch had been in the Warren family until it was sold in 1963 to a ranch operating company headed by Paul Etchepare of Denver. Etchepare, in turn, sold it to the

In 2005, Neil and Doris built a home at the Hat Six Ranch, where he raises Red Angus/Charolais cattle. Robert and Nancy McMurry run the livestock operation. ANN NOBLE PHOTO

McMurrys. The 120,000-acre sheep and cattle operation surrounds Cheyenne. The ranch was home to the Warhill sheep breed, developed by and named for Fred Warren, son of the Senator, and Professor John Hill at the University of Wyoming. The McMurrys continue to raise this breed of sheep on the ranch along with cattle. Susan McMurry Samuelson and her husband Doug live on and operate the Warren Ranch full-time for the McMurry family.

Back in Casper, in 2005, Neil and Doris built a home at the Hat Six Ranch. The home is located on the part of the ranch that continues to raise livestock. Neil's second cousin Robert McMurry and his wife Nancy operate the ranch, which runs Red Angus crossed with Charolais cattle. The feed is raised on three of Neil's ranches: the West Wind Farm near the Casper airport, the Hat Six Ranch, and the Alcova Ranch.

In addition to their home on the Hat Six, Neil possesses a structure of great nostalgic value. In 2002, when Mick McMurry was building the McMurry Medical Arts Center in downtown Casper, Neil's childhood home on Melrose Street was on the site of the development. Not wanting to tear down the house, Mick moved it to Neil's ranch at Hat Six. Neil likes to point out to visitors his childhood home, now situated close to his current home, and say, "This is where I started and this is where I've ended up."

Neil admits he does not need to earn any more money, yet he continues to work every day. "It's just something I have done all my life," says Neil. "It's just my lifestyle." Even his tax lawyer cannot slow him down. When Tom Long told Neil to stop making money because he would just have to pay more taxes, Neil said, "I've spent eighty-five years trying to make money. I have paid many taxes and I will continue to pay taxes." Neil goes on to say, "I don't hunt, fish, or play golf. I don't have any hobbies." In his mid-eighties, Neil regularly attends business meetings and continues to make his famous unannounced job site visits. And he shows no sign of slowing down. He continually talks about new business ideas and ventures. When discussing the recent work and future potential for the transloading facilities in Casper and Cheyenne, Neil says, "It's going to be a major, major project. I'm so goddamned excited about it, you can't believe it."

CHAD SORENSEN PHOTO

The house at 424 South Melrose: Otto McMurry's home in Casper, where Neil grew up, had become part of the Wyoming Medical Center. In 2002 it was in the path of the new McMurry Medical Arts Center and was in danger of being torn down. Mick moved the structure to Neil's ranch at Hat Six, seen at left.

CHAPTER 9
"PERSEVERANCE IS IMPORTANT" AND OTHER MCMURRY BUSINESS PRINCIPLES

Neil McMurry has always worked. As soon as he was old enough, Neil was delivering newspapers and taking on whatever jobs he could find, even during the Great Depression. Upon his return from Europe after serving his country in World War II, Neil immediately found work in construction and has remained in that line of business ever since. Exactly how many miles of Wyoming highway and interstate Neil and his company have built and rebuilt is unknown. The mileage is formidable, because every part of Wyoming has seen red and yellow Rissler and McMurry equipment operating on highways and bridges. McMurry Ready Mix continues to work on Wyoming highways today.

Neil's career has paralleled and been shaped by Wyoming's history and economy since the 1940s. In the aftermath of World War II, when the federal government was supporting Wyoming farmers and ranchers through a reservoir development program, Neil McMurry and Vern Rissler built the reservoirs. When the state needed highways and bridges, Rissler and McMurry Company constructed many of them. When the federal government supported the construction of the interstate system, Neil and Vern constructed many of the Wyoming sections.

In the 1950s, the United States opted to develop nuclear energy for military and non-military uses. This created a demand for uranium, a mineral found in Wyoming. Due to the federal government's interest in Wyoming's uranium industry, Neil and Vern expanded their business into uranium mining. In preparation for this mining, Neil obtained contracts to remove the overburden on the uranium ore throughout the state, including the Gas Hills and Shirley Basin, as well as out-of-state locations such as Maybell, Colorado. When the demand for uranium suddenly decreased with the accident at Three Mile Island in Pennsylvania, Rissler and McMurry Company's prospects in this industry faded along with Wyoming's.[1]

Throughout his busy construction career, Neil also pursued an interest in oil and gas drilling. Aware of Wyoming's mineral wealth and the nation's need for energy sources, Neil played a critical role in the successful development of the Jonah Field and the Pinedale Anticline, both huge natural gas reserves. Consistent with most of his career, Neil's timing was right, and his company implemented a successful drilling technique just as the demand for natural gas soared.

In explaining his business success, Neil is honest and witty. "I have found that no matter what you do, you have to work hard at it. You have to put in the hours and pay attention." When asked if that means working seven days a week, Neil responds, "Every once in a while, you have to work eight." Neil explains further, "You hire the smartest people you can to run your business. Then watch them and stay close to your business. You need to put in a lot of hours yourself, and always be available if they need you. Keep your ear tuned to what is going on."

Facing page: Neil and Doris seated at center, surrounded by Casper College students and their children who were recipients of McMurry Single Parent Scholarships in 2009. The program hosts an annual reception in honor of the McMurrys.

Neil at far right with his children in 2007. Left to right: Vic, Susan, Mick and Carol.

Another key to Neil's success is the strong relationships he builds with people, including his employees. In turn, many of his employees have great admiration for him. Long-time employee Joe Scott says, "Neil never asked me to do more than he would do." Neil has earned the trust of business cohorts, bankers, and Wyoming Department of Transportation staff. Many of these people built their careers together, trusting and respecting one another.

What sets Neil McMurry apart from many others in business is his perseverance. For example, when he was told that the Jonah Field and Pinedale Anticline were not economically viable for drilling natural gas, he, John Martin, and Mick were determined to figure out a way to make those reservoirs produce. Neil's daughter Carol speaks of her father's

can-do attitude. "It's never 'maybe I can do this,'" says Carol. When asked about the economic hard times, Neil responds, "It can throw you for a loop, but you never give up – you just keep going. That's the main thing." Carol adds, "my dad has nerves of steel."[2]

McMurry Oil Company partner John Martin points out that Neil "is a great entrepreneur and a great visionary. And he's a risk taker." Over and over again Neil has invested his personal money in enterprises he believed would work, and he has usually been right, though not always. He has never dwelled on the failures, but has immediately moved on to his next venture. Others attribute Neil's success to his knack for predicting the future. "He has the ability to see where things are going before other people do," claims Cheyenne lawyer Tom Long. "He's a true visionary," concludes Ron McMurry. "He accomplished what he did through hard work, risk, and ingenuity." Neil is by definition a true entrepreneur.

Having never attended college, and admittedly having paid little attention in high school, Neil acquired a less-than-formal education. "I had so many jobs that kept me up at night, I'd sleep in school," recalls Neil. Yet he became very knowledgeable about his businesses. For his construction work Neil learned everything he could about dirt, rocks, concrete, asphalt, and machinery, enabling him to make sound business decisions. He did the same for his work with McMurry Oil Company. He and his partners educated themselves as much as possible about oil and natural gas extraction.

Dan Guerttman, one of Neil's business partners, puts it this way. "Neil has the ability to dissect something, apply it where he thinks the world is going, and what the future might be." Tom Long explains, "I find Neil to have very astute business judgement. He has an excellent sense of where the forces of gravity are pulling people." Long also describes Neil as direct and focused during their meetings. "With Neil

I need to get to the point and in plain English," Long says, then adds, "I think Neil has little patience with lawyers! He always wants to get things done and get them done now!"

Others who have worked for Neil note that he has made them better workers. Current business partner Rich Fairservis says, "When you tell him something you better make sure it's accurate, because he'll remember it. He has a mind like a steel trap." Cary Brus was a banker when he first met Neil, and has attended meetings with him. "Neil can get to the heart of the problem faster than anyone else in the room," says Brus. "He listens better than anyone. You better be prepared because every once in a while he will, out of the blue, ask what you think. You can't just coast when you are with him. He made me a much better lender and banker."

In a *Casper Star-Tribune* letter to the editor published in 2000, David J. Crnich wrote, "Neil McMurry has been in business for 50 plus years and has made many more friends than enemies, and most persons who have either worked for him or dealt with him on any level have found a man who is fair, caring and willing to go the extra mile for his employees and business associates."[3] Behind his gruff exterior, Neil cares about his hard-working employees. He knows what his employees are going through because he has also done the work.

Neil is honest and expects the same from the people around him. His construction company is remembered for completing excellent work without cutting corners, resulting in hundreds of highway and interstate miles that were well-built and safe. Moreover, Neil never filed a claim against the state in the interest of financial gain, and he refused to participate in any bid-rigging for highway jobs. Years later, people in the highway construction industry note that Neil McMurry prevented bid-rigging in Wyoming. "He has the highest level of integrity," says Dan Guerttman.

Neil's sense of humor is notorious. Don Basko, Wyoming State Oil and Gas Supervisor, who worked with Neil as well as being his neighbor in Casper, says, "You'd ask him how things are going, and he would say, 'terrible! Wages are high and prices are low.' He was always giving the impression that he was going to starve to death and the company was going broke." Basko is describing yet another "McMurryism," the label invented by the Wyoming Highway Department's Leno Menghini. Dan Guerttman says, "Neil has an incredible sense of humor, and he always has a story for whatever the situation is. He has an incredible memory for stories and events."

It is impossible to accurately measure the impact Neil McMurry has had on Wyoming. As one of Wyoming's largest highway contractors, and later developing natural gas on the Jonah Field and Pinedale Anticline, he created thousands of jobs, made hundreds of careers, helped countless people pay for their educations or simply raise a family in Wyoming. His enterprises have significantly increased the infrastructure and the tax base wherever he has established them. Neil has always been dedicated to his home state. "He is very committed to Wyoming," says Bill Weeks, one of his investors in the Jonah Field.

Philanthropy in Wyoming

McMurry companies have always been generous, but with the profit from the sale of the Jonah Field and Pinedale Anticline leases, Neil has given even more to Wyoming despite the fact that many in the community have been very critical of him, especially the statewide newspaper, the *Casper Star-Tribune*.

Neil has always cared about those less fortunate, and he understands the needs of the working man and woman. Neil's financial assistance comes largely in the form of providing skills to enable workers to make a living wage and in good childcare, always important for working parents.

Throughout his career, Neil has recognized the importance of a trained workforce – a benefit not only for employers, but for employees as well. Neil greatly assisted in providing a training center for industry workers when he provided seed money to the Wyoming Contractors Association (WCA) Construction Careers Foundation. Charlie Ware, Executive Director of the WCA, started the foundation with fifty thousand dollars from Neil who then challenged the rest of the members to match it, and they did.

To assist with the building, loans were made available from the Wyoming Business Council, the Casper Area Economic Development Alliance, and Casper area banks. Individuals and corporations also contributed significantly to the building fund. The largest donors were members of the McMurry family, including Neil and Doris and all five of

The McMurry Regional Training Center.

Neil's children. The facility, therefore, was named for them. The Construction Careers Foundation owns the property and buildings, and the Wyoming Contractors Association rents the facility from the Foundation. The dedication and ribbon cutting ceremony for the McMurry Regional Training Center, located in north Casper on Bryan Stock Trail Road, was held on April 19, 2002.

WCA's McMurry Regional Training Center offers technical training for various industry trades. The facility is located on 38 acres and currently comprises two buildings which include classrooms, a computer training room, a shop with welding booths, and a 10-ton full-length overhead crane. On the grounds is a drilling rig and large equipment rented from Caterpillar for instruction. The Center explains in its literature, "We provide industry driven, short-term, high intensity training programs that allow our students to focus on developing knowledge and skills for a career in a high demand industry. Our customized and condensed training model allows us to keep training lengths short so that you can get a job and paycheck sooner without sacrificing quality or career!"[4]

Job placement is an important component of the McMurry Training Center. The center is proud of its high placement rate for those who complete its training programs. Again, according to its literature, "our industry partners are not only hiring our graduates, but are also investors in the programs and the training center itself. This unique relationship allows us to understand the employer's needs and hiring patterns at a ground floor level. This ensures that you are not only taking advantage of our training, but also our industry hiring network." By 2010, over sixteen thousand workers had received training at the McMurry Regional Training Center for jobs in the oil and gas industry, heavy equipment operation, truck driving, and occupational safety.

Neil and Doris have been very generous to Casper College. In 2000, they donated five million dollars to the college's Foundation. "It had a major impact at the time," says Paul Hallock, Executive Director of the Casper College Foundation. Three million dollars of the McMurry donation assisted with major renovation projects. One project overhauled a building, originally constructed in 1983, for workforce training. The building was renamed the Neil and Doris McMurry Career Studies Building, and is a complex of workshops and classrooms for instruction in automotive service and repair as well as diesel and natural gas power.

A portion of the funds also helped renovate the Casper College Center. A plaque with a picture of Ellie McMurry hangs in the renovated facilities. It reads in part: "The renovation of the College Center was funded by a gift given to honor the memory of Ellie McMurry. The five McMurry children attended Casper College. Ellie McMurry had a special place in her heart for young people who needed education and training. Casper College is deeply appreciative of the generosity and support of this outstanding family."

Doris and Neil at center, with Casper College Foundation Executive Director Paul Hallock at left and Casper College Student Success Coordinator Kym Byrd at right, marking their 2008 donation of one million dollars. MATT YOUNG, CASPER COLLEGE PHOTO

The Family Resource Center at Casper College, later renamed the Early Childhood Learning Center, received one million from the original five-million-dollar gift. This donation came at a time of financial difficulties, with the center slated to be closed. Not only was the program saved, it was expanded to include degreed teachers serving more children from birth through age six. A pre-school as well as a child care center, the Early Childhood Learning Center often reaches some of the most needy children in the area whose parents are pursuing their educations at Casper College. "Without the [McMurry] money I don't think that we would have been able to receive accreditation and keep it," says director Donna Sonesen. She adds that Neil's donation continues to assist with scholarships, facility upgrades, and educational materials.

The remaining one million dollars from Neil and Doris's donation initiated an endowment for Casper College's Single Parents Scholarship Program, which assists non-married students who have children. In 2009, qualifying students

received $1,100 a semester. The money can be used for rent, groceries, child care, or other expenses. In addition, an "emergency fund" covers critical unforeseen expenses the students may incur, such as a car repair or medical bill. "The students are so grateful for getting this money," says Kim Byrd, Student Success Coordinator and administrator of the program. "I don't think they could do it without that assistance."

The Casper College Single Parent Program and the Early Childhood Learning Center have been so successful that in 2008 Neil and Doris donated an additional one million dollars to further secure the endowment. This was matched dollar for dollar by the Wyoming Community College Endowment Challenge Matching Program, an endowment established by the Wyoming State Legislature in 2001. In announcing the award, Paul Hallock, Executive Director of the Casper College Foundation said, "Neil and Doris have been long-time supporters of our single parent students and we are grateful for their interest in the success of our students and this college. Ultimately the students are the beneficiaries and have the opportunity to accomplish their career goals as a result of the McMurrys' generosity."

One of the students who has participated in the Casper College Single Parent Program is Marty Wilson, a single mother of four children who received her nursing degree with help from the program. During the course of her studies, the McMurrys kept in touch with Marty, inviting her to dinner at the Hat Six truck stop, asking her about her life goals, following up

Top left: Children at the Early Childhood Learning Center hone their motor skills while pretending to roast marshmallows indoors.

Bottom left: Neil congratulates and encourages a Casper College student participating in the Single Parent Scholarship program he helped initiate.

on her progress, and encouraging her to complete her course work. Upon her graduation in 2002, Neil invited Marty to the McMurry home. During the visit, he handed her an envelope with a $1,000 check made out to her. "He said, 'Use it for whatever you want,'" recalls Marty. "At that time it was hard to clothe my kids, so I took them shopping."

In 2003, Neil had knee surgery at the Wyoming Medical Center in Casper. As luck would have it, his case manager on the surgical floor was Marty Wilson. Marty admits that she would not have been financially able to attend school without the Single Parent Program. "Through the program, Neil and Doris paid for my books and part of my child care, if I was running short," says Marty. While taking care of Neil at the hospital, Marty told him how much she appreciated his help, pointing out that she would not have become a nurse had it not been for his financial support. She also realized that his moral support had perhaps helped even more. "The thing that meant so much to me," says Marty, choking up, "was that they actually believed in me." The program is equally gratifying to Neil. "You can see results," he says. "So many [who have benefited from this program] have later thanked me."

Neil and his children have also been generous donors to the Child Development Center of Natrona County. Through recent contributions, the renovated facility on Twelfth Street continues to house a program which "exists to provide premier, family-focused, developmentally appropriate services for children from birth through age five." This project has particular significance for the family because this is where their mother Ellie had volunteered for years. Executive Director John Starnes says "Ellie's legacy lives on at the Center through the philanthropic giving of her family."[5]

In 2009, Neil and Doris gave the old Coliseum Motors building on Fifth and Wolcott in Casper to the 12-24 Club

During a reception for the McMurrys hosted by the 2010 Casper College Single Parent Scholarship Program, Neil enjoys a special presentation from the program's youngsters.

after the organization was evicted from its previous location. This gift, worth over a million dollars, became the new home for the Club, which provides a place where people recovering from any addiction can find help. The 12-24 Club, whose name stands for 12 steps of recovery 24 hours a day, is home to twenty-two dependence recovery organizations serving thousands of people annually. The remodeled building is big enough to house not only the 12-24 Club, but also some rental space that helps offset operating costs. Executive Director Dan Cantine credits Neil for making the new

building possible. "One of my personal highlights every week is when I call Neil to give a progress report," says Cantine. "He is always available, helpful, and encouraging. For a mutt like me to have this opportunity with him and his family is truly a blessing in my life."

It is no accident that through his generosity, Neil helps people who are hard working, facing challenges, and taking personal responsibility for their success – for these are all things that Neil understands personally. Following Neil's example, his children, business partners, and employees have also given generously in Wyoming. "We were born in Wyoming, and our parents raised us to give back to the state that gave us so much," says Susan McMurry Samuelson. Wyoming education, healthcare, libraries, and children's programs are just some of the beneficiaries of the McMurry community's spirit of generosity. "We are all the beneficiaries, either directly or indirectly, from what this family has done for the state," says Cary Brus, who has worked with Neil and Mick McMurry. "The McMurrys have the sense of obligation and commitment to give back." The impact from the success of the Jonah Field and Pinedale Anticline natural gas fields has been called the "Hand of Jonah" or the "Gift of Jonah" by those directly involved. That hand has reached far and wide across the state.

"In recognition of countless hours of support and service to the University of Wyoming and to their communities, the Doris and William N. 'Neil' McMurry family of Casper has

Top left: The Child Development Center of Natrona County provides services to children from birth to age five. This is the same program where Ellie McMurry volunteered for many years.

Bottom left: Governor Dave Freudenthal presents Neil McMurry with the 2004 Newell B. Sargent Spirit of Philanthropy Award.

been selected as the Wyoming Family of the Year," announced the University in 2002. The Associated Parents of the University of Wyoming selected the McMurrys for this honor based on their commitment and devotion to the University and the state. In 2004, Neil McMurry received the "Lifetime Achievement Award" from *The Wyoming Business Report* in conjunction with the Wyoming Business Council, the Wyoming Chamber of Commerce Executives and the Wyoming Economic Development Association for his long-time commitment to Wyoming's growth.

Also in 2004, Governor Dave Freudenthal presented Neil McMurry with the Newell B. Sargent Spirit of Philanthropy Award conferred by the Board of Directors of the Wyoming Community Foundation. At the award ceremony Governor Freudenthal said, "I commend him as a citizen who built the state's economy and as a philanthropist who builds the state's spirit."

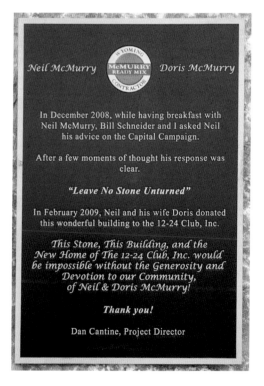

Clockwise from top left:
The old Coliseum Motors Building at Fifth and Wolcott in Casper has been renovated into a new facility for the 12-24 Club, a place where anyone recovering from an addiction can find help. The colors of the building are red and yellow, Neil's favorites.

Neil and Doris were honored at the 12-24 Club's grand opening in March 2010. They stand here with Lona and Dan Cantine, Executive Director.

A plaque honoring Neil and Doris is attached to a boulder in front of the 12-24 Club.

ACKNOWLEDGEMENTS

While the McMurry family has been very helpful and supportive of this project, most family members were at first somewhat apprehensive. They are not ones to seek attention. With the encouragement of Neil's younger son, Vic, the project proceeded – and we are all now glad that he kept pushing for this publication.

Writing the biography of Neil McMurry has been an honor and a pleasure. I began by spending a few days with Neil, age eighty-four when we started. He was recovering from back surgery and I was told that this had slowed him down. I had a hard time absorbing this, because we talked until midnight every night and he had the coffee on by five the next morning. Throughout the days and evenings he shared stories of his family and work, usually while driving to check on his various businesses. At every stop he had a conversation with his employees. He asked them about the business on that day, and he asked them about themselves. It was truly a pleasure watching these interactions.

Neil's children and wife Doris graciously provided interviews. Eldest daughter Carol was particularly helpful, as she has become the family archivist. Most of the family photographs in this book come from her collection. Sons Mick and Vic have vivid memories of their childhoods, as does youngest daughter Susan, and all of them added a different dimension of growing up as a child of Neil McMurry. Unfortunately, Neil's daughter Gayle passed away a year before the project began, but her lifetime friend Linda Pouttu helped fill in her story. Bucky Walker, a lifetime friend of Mick and Vic, also assisted with his McMurry family recollections.

Extended family members helped, too. Neil's sisters-in-law, Donna and Betty McMurry, and cousin Jim McMurry and his wife Alice, shared stories spanning decades of Neil's life, having known him since he was a young man. Younger relatives Pat and Ron McMurry were also great resources. They worked for Neil for many years and later became business partners.

Neil's World War II experience was further brought to life by two of his fellow army buddies. Raymond McMillan, a resident of Morgan, Utah, has kept in touch with Neil since their time in the military. Jim McNeil of Medford, Oregon, recently celebrated his ninety-third birthday with a visit from Neil.

Unfortunately, Neil's lifetime business partner, Vern Rissler, passed away in 1999; but Vern's son Jim filled in remarkably well. In addition to giving me hours on the telephone, Jim read and offered critical corrections and suggestions for several chapters. Three former directors of the Wyoming Department of Transportation, all of whom worked with Neil for many years, shared their memories: Don Diller, Leno Menghini, and Gene Roccabruna. The three men all told similar stories about Neil, including his incredibly strong work ethic and honesty, as well as comments about his special turns of phrase, for which Menghini coined the term "McMurryisms." Gus Fleischli, Bob Gaukel, and Charlie Ware, who worked with Neil during his years in construction, also assisted with this project.

The astounding story of southwest Wyoming's Jonah Field and Pinedale Anticline, and Neil's involvement in their rediscovery, was put together with assistance from John Martin, James Shaw, Joe Scott, Don Basko, and Cary Brus. Mick McMurry was particularly helpful in explaining the natural gas production process in general and in the Jonah Field and Pinedale Anticline in particular. Mick also provided the photographs for this chapter.

Neil's business career diversified in 2000 after he sold the McMurry Oil Company and its interest in the Jonah Field and Pinedale Anticline. He started several new companies, mainly in the Casper area. Rich Fairservis, Neil's partner in many of these later businesses, helped document this recent work.

Thousands of people have been the beneficiaries of Neil McMurry's generosity. Helping record this philanthropy was Press Stephens from the Wyoming Community Foundation, Paul Hallock of the Casper College Foundation, Dan Cantine of the 12-24 Club, and John Starnes of the Child Development Center of Natrona County. All spoke not only of Neil's financial assistance, but also of his moral support, which they equally appreciated.

Because Neil does a remarkable job of keeping in touch with people whom he has known throughout his life, his contacts were easy to locate. It speaks volumes of a man when everyone wants to talk about him. From his army comrades to his family members to his working partners and employees, all speak of Neil with utmost respect. I also thought it was interesting that everyone largely said the same thing about Neil. In every interview, I heard in one way or another, "he's a man of great integrity and honesty." Another frequent comment was that you had to get to know him in order to appreciate his unique sense of humor!

Vic's business associates and good friends Chad and Tammy Sorensen were critical throughout the whole process. I also thank Neil's business partner Dan Guerttman for his constant assistance throughout this project, as well as long-time family friend Bucky Walker, who literally went all over Casper collecting pictures and information for me. Linda Slattery, Neil and Doris' secretary, gave help and moral support throughout. Kevin Anderson, Western History Archivist at the Casper College History Center, assisted with research and photographs. Thanks also to Faith Bolen who transcribed all the interviews.

My editors were the best, starting with my husband, David, who read and re-read all of the chapters several times and made good suggestions. My brother, Wally Chambers, also offered important corrections and comments. My editing team of Sue Sommers and Dari Quirk played a critical role in this book. They took a personal interest in this story. Sue Sommers also is the book's designer.

Special thanks to Vic McMurry for his insight and perseverance. I am also grateful to Vic for his kindness and friendship throughout the project. I have thoroughly enjoyed writing this book and getting to know a wonderful Wyoming family who has done great things for the state. But the best part has been the opportunity to get to know Neil McMurry, a truly remarkable individual.

— *Ann Chambers Noble*

NOTES

Chapter 1
Young Neil McMurry

1   Otto McMurry was born September 25, 1900. Alma Doke McMurry was born February 25, 1901.

2   *Wyoming; A Guide to Its History, Highways, and People.* Compiled by workers of the Writers' Program of the Work Projects Administration in the State of Wyoming (New York: Oxford University Press, 1941; repr. Lincoln: University of Nebraska Press, 1981), 173-182. The American Guide Series was a product of the Writers' Program of the Work Projects Administration, a New Deal program during the Great Depression designed to give useful employment to research workers and writers.

Chapter 2
The World at War: Neil's Generation

1   Hugh McGregor was born December 7, 1901; his wife Stella was born May 9, 1899 in Junction City, Kansas.

2   "Rosie the Riveter" was a nickname applied to the women who took manufacturing jobs that supported the war effort, during World War II. So many men had been enlisted into the military that these important jobs, which normally would have been filled by men, went to women instead.

Chapter 3
Reservoirs, Highways, Bridges and Interstates:
The Rissler and McMurry Company

1   *Casper Star-Tribune*, Advertising Supplement, Summer, 1995. The newspaper listed this date as 1944, but the correct year is 1946. Newspaper quotes throughout this chapter refer to this supplement.

2   Ibid.

3   Don Diller became the first director in July 1991 when Wyoming state government reorganization went into effect.

4   Gene Roccabruna would later become the Second Director for the Wyoming Department of Transportation, following Don Diller.

5   The Goose Egg is a historic family restaurant and ranch located five miles southwest of Casper on Highway 220. The Goose Egg Ranch was made famous by Owen Wister's book, *The Virginian.*

Chapter 4
Neil and Ellie Raising a Family

1   The Servicemen's Readjustment Act of 1944, commonly known as the G.I. Bill of Rights, offered home loan guaranties from 1944 to 1952 and was administered by the Veterans Administration (VA). It backed nearly 2.4 million home loans for World War II veterans.

2   Brendan Phipps, M.D., et al, "The Casper Project – An Enforced Mass-Culture Streptococcic Control Program," *The Journal of the American Medical Association* 166, no. 10 (March 8, 1958): 1113.

3   *The Greeley Tribune*, August 2, 1960.

Chapter 5
Neil and Ellie's Children Become Adults

1   A drafted soldier during the Vietnam War was required to serve twenty-four months in active duty. After four months of basic and advanced training, Mick served twelve months combat duty in Vietnam. He was then given the opportunity to be honorably discharged early (after a total of nineteen months) if he extended his combat tour an additional three months. This he opted to do.

2   Irwin was nicknamed by his uncles after the Barney Google comic strip character "Jug" or "Jughaid," who always wore a coonskin cap and suspenders. The comic strip, created in 1919 by Billy DeBeck, featured southern Appalachian hillbillies.

Chapter 6
Rissler and McMurry Company After 1980: A New Era

1   *Casper Star-Tribune*, December 19, 1990.

2   *Casper Star-Tribune*, November 8, 1990; September 24, 1991.

3   The leader of Friends of Bessemer Mountain was Cathy Killean, who wrote about this event in a self-published book, *To Save A Mountain*, 1997.

4   *Casper Star-Tribune*, February 5, 1992; April 18, 1992; April 22, 1993; July 3, 1993.

5   *Casper Star-Tribune,* October 18, 1990.

6   Ibid.

7   *Casper Star-Tribune*, January 28, 1993; February 4, 1993.

8   *Casper Star-Tribune,* December 8, 1995; December 20, 1995; February 24, 1996; June 6, 1996; October 16, 1996.

Chapter 7
A Little Company in a Big Field: The McMurry Oil Company in the Jonah Field and Pinedale Anticline

1   An override is an interest and royalty in the oil, gas, or minerals extracted from another's land that is carved out of the producer's working interest and is not tied to production costs.

2   Jim Urbigkit, "The Jonah Story," *Sublette County Journal,* January 31, 1998. The series appeared December 31, 1997, January 31, 1998 (incorrectly labeled 1997), and February 27, 1998.

3   Ibid.

4   A farm-in, or carried interest, is usually a buy-in for one-third payment of the total cost in exchange for one-fourth ownership.

5   Urbigkit, "The Jonah Story," January 31, 1998.

6   Susan Klann, "Jonah's Tale," Hart Publications, Inc., Houston, TX, 1997. Periodical unknown, clipping from McMurry files.

7   *Casper Star-Tribune*, November 10, 2001.

8   "Sublette County Socioeconomics," website produced for the Sublette County Partnership. Michael S. Coburn, Socioeconomic Analyst. Accessed at http://sublette-se.org/Jonah.

9   Nitrogen oxide (NOx) is the collective label for a group of highly reactive gasses covered by the Environmental Protection Agency's National Ambient Air Quality Standard. Different forms of NOx (notably nitrogen dioxide, or NO_2) can arise quickly from the emissions of cars, trucks and buses, power plants, and off-road equipment. In addition to contributing to the formation of ground-level ozone and fine particle pollution, NO_2 is linked to a number of adverse effects on the respiratory system.

10 *Casper Star-Tribune*, October 17, 1999.

11 Urbigkit, "The Jonah Story," January 31, 1998.

Chapter 8
Neil McMurry's 21st-Century Businesses

1   *Casper Star-Tribune*, September 22, 2000.

2   *Casper Star-Tribune*, June 22, 2008.

3   Bishop Industrial Rail Park, LLC is majority owned by Neil McMurry and Rich Fairservis, with Dan Guerttman, Robert West, Ron McMurry, and Pat McMurry.

4   Wyoming Business Council, www.wyomingbusiness.org, "Natrona County Projects," Accessed January 2008.

5   *Casper Star-Tribune*, January 10, 2010.

Chapter 9
"Perseverance is Important" and Other McMurry Business Principles

1   In 1979, Three Mile Island Nuclear Generating Station in Pennsylvania was the site of an industrial accident involving a partial core meltdown. It was the most serious accident in U.S. commercial nuclear power plant operating history. Although there were no serious injuries, the accident had a profound, negative, and immediate effect on nuclear energy, bringing it largely to a halt.

2   *Made in Wyoming: Our Legacy of Success* (Casper, WY: Casper Star-Tribune Communications, 2007), 58.

3   *Casper Star-Tribune*, July 7, 2000.

4   The source for all quotes about the McMurry Training Center is www.mcmurrytrainingcenter.com.

5   Mission statement for the Child Development Center of Natrona County, 2010.

BIBLIOGRAPHY

Oral Interviews by Ann Chambers Noble

Basko, Don. January 24, 2010; via telephone, Casper, Wyoming.

Byrd, Kim. March 26, 2009; Casper, Wyoming.

Brownlee, Dyce. June 23, 2009; Alcova, Wyoming.

Brus, Cary. December 8, 2008; Casper, Wyoming.

Cordingly, Kurt. August 14, 2008; Pinedale, Wyoming.

Diller, Don. October 11, 2008; Cheyenne, Wyoming.

Fairservis, Rich. September 28, 2008; Casper, Wyoming.

Fleischli, Gus. April 1, 2009; via telephone, Cheyenne, Wyoming.

Gaukel, Robert. January 28, 2009; Loveland, Colorado.

Guerttman, Dan. July 9, 2008; Casper, Wyoming.

Hallock, Paul. March 26, 2009; Casper, Wyoming.

Hurley, G. William. September 27, 2008; Casper, Wyoming.

Long, Tom. March 10, 2009; Cheyenne, Wyoming.

Martin, John. January 27, 2009; Greenwood Village, Colorado.

McMillan, Raymond. November 2, 2008; Morgan, Utah.

McMurry, Betty. June 17, 2008; Bar Nunn, Wyoming.

McMurry, Carol. March 9 & 10, 2009; Loveland, Colorado.

McMurry, Donna. September 27, 2008; Casper, Wyoming.

McMurry, Doris. March 27, 2009; Casper, Wyoming.

McMurry, Jim and Alice. June 15, 2008; Casper, Wyoming.

McMurry, Neil Albert "Mick." December 8, 2008; Casper, Wyoming.

McMurry, Pat. July 9, 2008; Casper, Wyoming.

McMurry, Ronald. December 7, 2008; Casper, Wyoming.

McMurry, Victor. December 4 & 5, 2008; Cora, Wyoming.

McMurry, William Neil. March 28, 29, 30, 2008; Casper, Wyoming. December 7 & 9, 2008; Casper, Wyoming. March 26, 2009; Casper, Wyoming. April 21, 2009; Casper, Wyoming. May 26, 2009; Pinedale, Wyoming.

McNeil, Jim. November 10, 2008; via telephone.

Menghini, Leno. October 10, 2008; Cheyenne, Wyoming.

Pouttu, Linda Schumacher. August 14, 2008; Pinedale, Wyoming.

Rissler, Jim. January 5, 2009; via telephone.

Roccabruna, Gene. October 11, 2008; Cheyenne, Wyoming.

Samuelson, Susan McMurry. March 10, 2009.

Scott, Joe. December 8, 2008; Casper, Wyoming.

Shaw, James. August 15, 2008; Pinedale, Wyoming.

Sonesen, Donna. March 26, 2009; Capser, Wyoming.

Walker, Bucky. December 8, 2008; Casper, Wyoming.

Ware, Charlie. October 12, 2008; Cheyenne, Wyoming.

Weeks, Bill. January 27, 2009; Denver, Colorado.

Wilson, Marty. April 30, 2009; via telephone.

Sources Consulted

Federal Writers' Project. *Wyoming; A Guide to Its History, Highways, and People.* Compiled by workers of the Writers' Program of the Work Projects Administration in the State of Wyoming, Sponsored by Dr. Lester C. Hunt, Secretary of State. New York: Oxford University Press, 1941. Reprinted Lincoln: University of Nebraska Press, 1981. Page references are to the 1981 edition.

Hyne, Norman J., Ph.D. *Nontechnical Guide to Petroleum Geology, Exploration, Drilling and Production*, Tulsa: PennWell Books, 1995.

Larson, T. A. *History of Wyoming.* Lincoln: University of Nebraska Press, 1965.

Ropp, Theodore. "World War II." *The World Book Encyclopedia.* Field Enterprises Educational Corporation, 1976.

Sulzberger, C. L. *The American Heritage Picture History of World War II.* New York: Crown Publishers, Inc., 1966.

Urbigkit, Jim. "The Jonah Story," *Sublette County Journal,* December 31, 1997, January 31, 1998, February 27, 1998.

Aerial view of the Standard Oil Refinery, Casper, Wyoming, 1920. BLACKMORE COLLECTION, CASPER COLLEGE WESTERN HISTORY CENTER

Index